Sublimation Crafting

Sublimation Crafting

The Ultimate DIY Guide to Printing and Pressing **Vibrant** Tumblers, T-shirts, Home Décor, and More

Cori George

BETTER DAY BOOKS®

HAPPY · CREATIVE · CURATED

Learn more about sublimation printing and
all the resources I mention in this book at
www.sublimationcrafting.com

Download all the designs used
in this book at
**www.betterdaybooks.com/
sublimation-crafting-png-download**

Sublimation Crafting © 2024 by Cori George and
Better Day Books, Inc.

Publisher: Peg Couch
Book Designer: Llara Pazdan
Cover Designer: Ashlee Wadeson
Editor: Colleen Dorsey
Photo Stylist (finished projects): Lori Wenger
Photographer (finished projects): Jason Masters
Photographer (step-by-step and other): Cori George

Additional photo credits: photo on pages 8–9: Stephanie Dandini
Photography; photos on pages 15, 61, 161: Kathryn Moran Photography;
photo on page 26: Sawgrass

Library of Congress Control Number: 2023945569
ISBN: 978-0-7643-6799-1
Printed in China
10 9 8 7 6 5 4 3 2 1

Copublished by Better Day Books, Inc., and Schiffer Publishing, Ltd.

Better Day Books
P.O. Box 21462
York, PA 17402
Phone: 717-487-5523
Email: hello@betterdaybooks.com
www.betterdaybooks.com
@better_day_books

Schiffer Publishing
4880 Lower Valley Road
Atglen, PA 19310
Phone: 610-593-1777
Fax: 610-593-2002
Email: info@schifferbooks.com
www.schifferbooks.com

This title is available for promotional or commercial use,
including special editions. Contact info@schifferbooks.com
for more information.

To all of my boys.
I love being on this
adventure with you.

Contents

Part 1: Learning about Sublimation

88

96

84

104

116

150

Welcome

Hey hey!

Welcome to the wonderful, creative world of sublimation crafting! With sublimation, you can transfer vivid, full-color permanent images to a wide range of blank items, including apparel, drinkware, gift ideas, and more. You can make incredible things with sublimation, but starting out can be intimidating. I'm here to help!

This book includes step-by-step instructions for the everyday crafter. No confusing terms or technical knowledge are needed—just everything you need to get started with sublimation crafting. We'll start with an overview of sublimation, then discuss sublimation printer options. We'll talk about the tools and supplies you'll need and the process of setting up a sublimation project. Then we'll use what we've learned to make 18 fun projects, each designed to teach you unique sublimation skills. Plus, we'll cover a range of issues and how you might troubleshoot them.

Be encouraged as you're learning these new skills! You're bound to make mistakes. You will mess up something, and things won't always go as you expect. Don't take it personally—keep practicing. I've had a ton of "craft fails" in my journey as a sublimation crafter. It's all part of the process. With the tips in this book, you can minimize those difficulties, but don't be too hard on yourself if something doesn't go right the first time.

Give yourself permission to experiment. Give yourself permission to fail. You'll learn something new with every mistake. It's all part of the learning process! Your successes will soon far outweigh your failures, and you'll be a confident sublimation crafter.

Happy crafting!

Top 10 Reasons Sublimation Crafting Is Special

VIBRANT PRINTS THAT LAST:

Sublimation gives you stunning, vibrant, long-lasting prints that won't crack, fade, or peel over time.

ENDLESS PROJECT POSSIBILITIES:

Whether it's polyester fabrics, ceramic, neoprene, metal, or even glass, sublimation works on a wide range of blanks.

NO TEXTURE OR FEEL:

Unlike other methods, sublimation prints are infused directly into the material, leaving no added texture or feel to your image.

FULL-COLOR PRINTS:

Unlike HTV, you can print intricate designs with an unlimited color palette, giving you endless design possibilities.

PERFECT FOR GIFTS:

Customize a huge range of blanks to create personalized and meaningful gifts that will make your loved ones feel special.

SCALES UP FOR YOUR SMALL BUSINESS:

Sublimation is ideal for producing small batches of custom items, making it perfect for craft fairs or your online shop.

WASHABLE AND DURABLE:

Because sublimation is permanent, your projects can withstand washing and daily use, making sublimation perfect for custom clothing, drinkware, and more.

GREAT FOR EVENTS:

It's so easy to make personalized merch for weddings, team events, kids' school activities, family reunions, and more.

QUICK PRODUCTION TIME:

Most projects are just print and press, allowing you to create more projects in less time. No cutting, weeding, transfer tape, or other processes needed!

EXPANDS YOUR SKILLS:

Sublimation is a great "next step" if you already enjoy Cricut/cutting machines. Just add a sublimation printer and use the heat press you already have for your Cricut crafting.

38 Ready-to-Use Designs!

Every design featured in the projects in this book is available for you to download for free! Each file is provided as a PNG and is easy to multiply, modify, and customize in your chosen design software. Visit www.betterdaybooks.com/sublimation-crafting-png-download to download your files!

BE KIND

SUNSHINE

     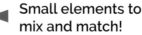

Small elements to mix and match!

MAKE WAVES

GOOD VIBES ONLY

THE SECRET INGREDIENT IS ALWAYS LOVE

Customizable designs for coasters and more!

▲ **Cool patterns for large designs!**

Quotes in fun fonts! ▼

Meet the Author

How did you first get into crafting? Have you always been creative?

I come from a creative family! My grandma made handmade cards, my mom sews purses and has her own Etsy shop, and my dad is a photographer. My mom taught me to sew when I was young, and I also loved everything crafty in the '90s: puff paint, spirograph, spin art, and friendship bracelets. Since then, I've never lost that love of crafting, and I'm hoping to pass that creative passion along to my boys.

How did you develop your personal design style?

Before I started crafting full time, I worked for a marketing agency. I learned what it takes to create a strong visual brand and I applied that to my own work! While my style is very bright and colorful, I'm also drawn to simplicity and clean lines. In particular, I love Scandinavian design and the use of solid colors and simple motifs. You won't find shabby chic farmhouse or grungy industrial themes in my work. I also love humor and whimsy—I truly love when I can make someone smile!

What advice can you give readers who want to spend more time in the craft room?

Start looking at crafting time as mandatory instead of just something you do in the margins! I don't want to spend too much time away from my family, so I've started involving my boys. Whether we're crafting something together or I've set them up with their own supplies while I work on my own project, it's a great way to spend time together and to instill in them a love of crafting and being creative. Recently we've crafted superhero capes for their stuffed animals, shirts for school spirit week, and Halloween costumes made from simple hoodies.

Your work exudes such positivity. What do you love most about crafting?

I've struggled with depression, and I've found that carving out a space for crafting and creativity has helped renew a sense of purpose and joy in my life—even if it's something as simple as finishing a page in a coloring book or making a card for a friend. While I'm a big fan of therapy and medication (I'm personally thankful for both!), working with my hands and creating something new is also good for my mental health. The world can be a dark and heavy place, so crafting beauty and spreading joy can be one small way to push back against that darkness.

What are your favorite things to craft?

I love anything that involves "crafting tech." So my favorite crafts are done using my Cricut machine, sublimation printer, laser cutter, and heat presses. I love that intersection of tech and crafting—designing something on my computer and then watching it come to life with the help of one of my machines.

Do you listen to music/podcasts while you work?

I'm actually a huge audiobook fan! When I'm crafting, I'll often have a novel playing in the background. I'll listen to just about any book, but my favorite genres are cozy murder mysteries and fantasy. When I'm at my computer, however, I prefer to work in silence—I find it easier to concentrate.

Besides crafting, what are your passions?

I absolutely love being outside with my husband, our twin boys, and our absolutely enormous Bernese mountain dog. We live in the beautiful Pacific Northwest and enjoy hiking, kayaking, and exploring our town. I'm also an avid reader (if the weather is nice, you'll probably find me on our deck with a book and cup of coffee!), and I always have a jigsaw puzzle going.

What do you hope readers will get from this book?

I hope readers will understand that it's okay to make mistakes while learning sublimation! There are a lot of variables involved, and sometimes things don't turn out like you think they will. Make some adjustments and try again. Mistakes are absolutely not failures—they are just part of the learning process.

What's next for you?

Lately I've been exploring "what's next" after sublimation! Sublimation is incredibly versatile, but, as you'll see, it does have some limitations. So while it's considerably more expensive, I've been exploring DTF (direct to film) printing and white toner printing as the next step up after sublimation.

Is there anything else you'd like to share?

Creativity looks different for everybody! Don't waste time comparing yourself to other people. You are allowed to love what you love, even if it's not trendy or liked by everyone. There are millions of sublimation images and projects out there—I know you will find some that you love!

Cori George is the owner and creative director of Hey, Let's Make Stuff! She is an author, maker, and entrepreneur who is passionate about creating content that is accessible and fun for every level of crafter. Based in Washington State, she loves inspiring half a million women every month to make their lives more fun with easy crafts, digital downloads, and simple DIY tutorials. She has partnered with Martha Stewart, Parade, Today, Good Housekeeping, Cricut, Apartment Therapy, Country Living, JOANN, and Buzzfeed. When she's not crafting, she loves traveling, strong coffee, and spending quality time with her husband and adorable twin boys. Her first book, *Paper Party*, was released by Leisure Arts in 2018, and her second book, *Easy Cricut Crafts*, was released by Better Day Books in 2022. Learn more at www.heyletsmakestuff.com and @heyletsmakestuff on Instagram. If you have any questions about the PNG files in this book, please email help@heyletsmakestuff.com.

CHECK OUT
EASY CRICUT® CRAFTS!

Inside this book also written by Cori, you'll find tons of simple cutting-machine projects for home décor, parties, kids, and organization. Each project comes with downloadable SVG files and works with many brands of cutting machines. Find the book at your preferred retailer or bookseller (ISBN: 978-0-7643-6548-5)!

Learning about Sublimation

Are you excited to get started on this super-satisfying sublimation journey? In the following pages, we'll go over everything you need to know about sublimation, from tools and materials to machines, software, and "sublimation sandwiches." You'll be ready to make stuff in no time!

What Is Sublimation?

If you're reading this, you may already know a little bit about sublimation, but understanding the theory well will set you up for success.

The Science of Sublimation

Let's start with a quick elementary school science lesson to help you understand what's actually happening in the sublimation process.

Think about water and its three states of matter: ice (solid), water (liquid), and steam (gas). We often think of states of matter like these moving in two directions:

- Solid to liquid to gas (through melting and then boiling/vaporizing)
- Gas to liquid to solid (through condensing and then freezing)

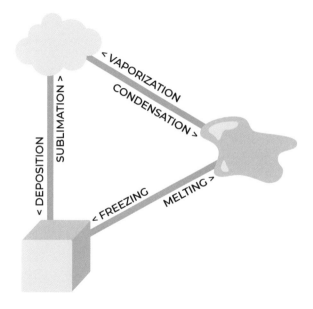

But there's more! You can go from a solid directly to a gas in a process known as sublimation. (You can also go from a gas directly to a solid, in a process called deposition—which is how frost forms on your car on a cold morning.)

In simplest terms, you'll print your design using a sublimation printer and then use high heat to turn the solid ink on the paper directly into a gas, which then bonds with your blank substrate, like a T-shirt or the sublimation coating on a mug.

This scientific process yields permanent, vibrant images that won't crack, fade, or peel no matter how many times you wash your project!

A sublimated design (bottom) and a heat-transfer vinyl design (top). Note how the HTV design is simply sitting on top of the fabric.

This permanence is what makes sublimation different from other products, such as heat-transfer vinyl (HTV). Instead of sitting on top of the substrate, sublimation actually bonds the ink into the substrate itself.

Safety First

Now that you know a bit of the science behind sublimation, let's talk safety. This information does not constitute medical advice, and you are responsible for your own decisions when it comes to sublimation and safety measures.

When the solid ink turns into a gas during sublimation, some of that gas ends up in the air and you may breathe it in. Certain blank substrates, like neoprene, create gases and odors of their own as well.

These fumes may be harmful if inhaled, particularly if you're prone to lung issues, headaches, and other health concerns.

Always work on sublimation crafts in a well-ventilated area. Consider setting up an air purifier near your sublimation work area. Wearing a respirator mask may help filter out these particles as well.

If you have concerns, talk to your doctor or other qualified medical professional.

Sublimation Printer Options

The basic starting point for any crafter's sublimation journey is to get their hands on a printer to start printing sublimation transfers!

There are two main printer options for sublimation. The first is using a sublimation-specific printer, and the second is to "convert" a regular printer for sublimation. (Converting is done by putting sublimation ink in a suitable printer, like an Epson EcoTank printer.) Let's take a look at the pros and cons of each option.

HARDWARE AND INK COSTS

Sublimation-Specific Printer

Sublimation printers are the more expensive option. Both the printer and the ink cost more because they are specifically designed for sublimation. You get the quality and expertise that comes from a company that understands sublimation printing. The most popular sublimation-specific printers, at the time of printing, are the Sawgrass SG500/SG1000 and the Epson F170/F570.

Converted Printer

Inkjet printers are much less expensive than sublimation-specific printers (often half the price), which makes them a popular option for hobby crafters beginning their sublimation journey. With the lower price comes a printer not specifically designed for sublimation. This can have quite an impact on your crafting, as you'll see.

Start with a new Epson EcoTank printer. Do not fill the printer with the normal Epson ink that comes with the printer. Instead, fill the printer with third-party sublimation ink designed for an Epson EcoTank printer. Converting a previously used printer for sublimation is a complex project and outside the scope of this book.

TECHNICAL SUPPORT

Sublimation-Specific Printer

With a sublimation-specific printer, you'll have access to the printer manufacturer's customer support team. If you have an issue with setup, you can contact support and they will walk you through any issues.

Converted Printer

You won't receive manufacturer support with a converted inkjet printer because the printer is not meant for sublimation. Once you convert it, you void the warranty and support won't be available.

The good news is that is online support groups can help if you're struggling! There are lots of people with real-life experience in these groups, and you can usually find help quickly and easily.

COLOR MANAGEMENT

Sublimation-Specific Printer

Color management can be tricky . . . but not if you have a sublimation-specific printer! Color management is built into the printer. You should not need to install and fumble with color profiles or other color management settings.

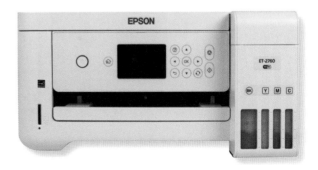

A Sawgrass SG500 sublimation-specific printer.

An Epson EcoTank printer that can be "converted" into a sublimation printer.

With a Sawgrass printer in particular, you can also choose specific substrates when printing, which affects the color profile. For example, if you choose neoprene (which is more absorbent), it will lay more ink down than if you choose hardboard (which is nonabsorbent). These profiles also adjust the color to the different "white points" of various blanks, since not every white is the same.

Converted Printer

Color management on a converted printer can be a struggle. Some crafters have great color without making any tweaks, while others have a difficult time getting correct colors. Often, you'll need to install an ICC profile on your printer to help manage the color. Even then, you may experience different results based on your substrate/blank, type of heat press you're using, humidity in your craft room, age of your ink, and more. Depending on your setup, you may find yourself doing a lot of testing to get your prints to look the best.

SOFTWARE

Sublimation-Specific Printer

With a Sawgrass printer, you'll have access to Sawgrass's free software programs DesignMate and PrintMate. You can also use other graphic design programs—like Adobe Photoshop or Corel Draw—if you'd like.

DesignMate comes with sublimation templates for many popular blanks/substrates. It's simple to design or upload an image and know you're getting the sizing just right. No guessing or other design programs needed!

PrintMate is an even more simplified printing solution for designs created in other programs. Just upload your design, make a few selections regarding size and substrate, and print.

Epson's F170/F570 sublimation printers do not have built-in software, so they are more like a converted printer (read on).

Converted Printer

While converted printers don't come with specific design software, you can use whatever graphic design program you're most comfortable with. This may be a pro or a con, depending on how familiar you are with different software programs.

MAINTENANCE

Sublimation-Specific Printer

With a Sawgrass printer, as long as you keep it powered on, very little (if any) manual maintenance is required. The printer will automatically perform periodic routine print head cleaning. While this does use some extra ink, it helps prevent clogging.

An Epson F170/F570 sublimation printer needs consistent use and to have its printer heads cleaned manually, just like a converted printer (read on).

Converted Printer

If you convert a printer, you will want to print regularly—at least once a week. You may need to clean your printer heads from time to time if you find the ink has clogged. Thankfully, this is a fairly simple process. If you don't print often or periodically clean your printer heads, your printer may become irreparably clogged and you'll have to buy a new printer. Consistent use is the best way to prevent head clogs with a converted printer.

What's the Right Printer for You?

Many factors go into choosing a printer, including your budget, experience level, and whether you plan to sell products. You'll find that most sublimation hobby crafters use a converted printer simply because there's a lower cost to getting started. Those looking for a more professional sublimation crafting experience or folks who want to start a small business often upgrade to a sublimation-specific printer.

To make things straightforward for this book, I will be using a Sawgrass SG1000 sublimation-specific printer with Sawgrass UHD inks, Sawgrass software, and both Sawgrass TruPix sublimation paper and A-Sub sublimation paper. There are also two tutorials where I use Cricut Design Space to take advantage of the Print Then Cut feature.

That being said, all the projects in this book can be made with a sublimation-specific printer or with a converted Epson EcoTank printer. If you'd like more information on converting an Epson EcoTank printer for sublimation, along with color management, maintenance, and other details, please visit the Sublimation Resources web link on page 4.

Sublimation Heat Press Comparison

Let's compare the many different heat presses that you can use to sublimate your transfers onto your projects.

In addition to a printer, you'll need a heat press to activate the sublimation ink and transfer your image to your blank substrate. There are many types of heat presses, and not every heat press works with every type of substrate. One type of heat press may be right for one crafter but may not work well for another. It truly depends on what kind of sublimation projects you'd like to create, as well as your space and budget.

The various parts of any heat press may get very hot, including the outside of the machine. Most sublimation projects take place at 360°F–400°F (182°C–205°C), and you don't want to be on the receiving end of that heat. A heat press also takes a long time to cool down, so be aware of that too.

Traditional Heat Press

There are two types of traditional heat presses: the swing-away press and the clamshell press. These types of heat press machines are the best for flat items, such as apparel, tote bags, coasters, ornaments, jigsaw puzzles, metal signs, and more.

SWING-AWAY HEAT PRESS

The top heat platen of a swing-away heat press is on a center column; the column swings the heating element away from the bottom plate. This kind of heat press requires more room than a clamshell press, since you need room to swing the top plate to the side, but it gives you more room to set up your project without your hands getting close to the hot platen. Swing-away presses also press more evenly, since the top platen is dropped vertically on top of your project and can adjust to thicker projects more easily.

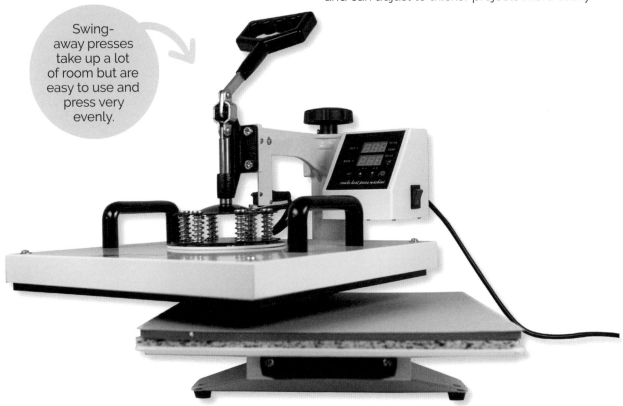

Swing-away presses take up a lot of room but are easy to use and press very evenly.

CLAMSHELL HEAT PRESS

A clamshell heat press operates with a hinge. The hinge is in the back and the top platen opens about 70° above the flat bottom plate. Some clamshell presses have a bottom plate that pulls out like a drawer so you can more easily place your project for pressing.

Most clamshell presses don't press from the top down completely flat. Due to this design, they aren't quite as adept at handling thicker objects because they tend to "squeeze" the project out from one end as they press—similar to how you would squeeze a tube of toothpaste. A clamshell press is great option if you're more limited on space or you aren't interested in pressing thicker projects.

AUTO HEAT PRESSES

There are also several "automatic" heat presses on the market, including the Cricut AutoPress and the Vevor Auto Heat Press. These presses automatically apply pressure instead of you adjusting it manually with a knob. While these presses can handle most sublimation projects, they may not produce good results with projects that require heavier pressure, including sublimation slates, tiles, glass cutting boards, and similar substrates.

HEAT PRESS ATTACHMENTS

Some traditional heat presses come with attachments so you can make more using your press. For example, my swing-away heat press has attachments for mugs, hats/caps, and two sizes of plates. This expands the capabilities of your heat press without needing other full-size machines.

Clamshell presses are a solid choice, especially if you have limited space.

Auto heat presses apply pressure automatically but, for that reason, may not be a good choice for projects requiring heavier pressure.

Cricut EasyPress

The Cricut EasyPress is a great option for crafters who are beginning their sublimation journey and find a traditional heat press intimidating. You will need an EasyPress 2 or EasyPress 3—the original EasyPress doesn't get hot enough for sublimation. The EasyPress is more portable and takes up significantly less space than a traditional heat press, so it's also great for smaller spaces.

Similar to a traditional heat press, the EasyPress can only press flat items that need light or medium pressure. It doesn't do well with heavy-pressure substrates. Many professional sublimation shops and bloggers dismiss the EasyPress, but I've found it capable for many common sublimation projects and recommend it for beginners if a traditional press is out of your price range or is too intimidating.

A Cricut EasyPress is a great starter press that has a more limited scope but still does a great job— and is very unintimidating!

Specialty Presses

If you're looking to press substrates that are not flat, you'll want a specialty press.

MUG PRESS

A mug press is designed to press mugs and other similarly shaped substrates, often with interchangeable heating elements for different-sized substrates. Cricut also has a sleek mug press that many find less intimidating than a traditional mug press. The time and temperature settings are both built into the press—you don't need to set them manually. The biggest downside is that there are a limited number of mug shapes and sizes you can use.

TUMBLER PRESS

Most tumbler presses have interchangeable heating elements, meaning you can press a wide range of drinkware. This includes not just tumblers but also mugs and glassware.

OTHER SPECIALTY PRESSES

Additionally, there are other specialty heat presses and attachments for doing projects such as hats, shoes, plates, and more.

A mug press is the easiest way to create mugs and similarly shaped items.

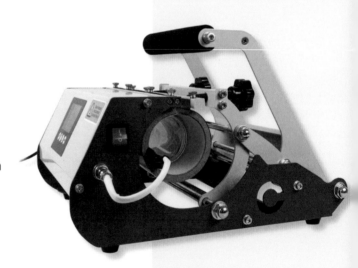

A tumbler press may look complicated, but it makes creating tumblers and other drinkware a cinch.

Convection Oven or Air Fryer

A convection oven or air fryer can be a less expensive heat source for mugs, tumblers, and oddly shaped blanks like wine glasses and pet dishes. You'll use specialty shrink-wrap or silicone sleeves to mimic the pressure of a heat press inside the oven.

Do not use the same convection oven for food and sublimation. As mentioned at the beginning of this book, sublimation ink is turned into a gas during the sublimation process. These noxious gases will remain in your oven and can make their way into your food if you use the same oven for both. Purchase a separate convection oven or air fryer to use only for sublimation; never use your main home oven.

If you don't want to get a specialty mug or tumbler press, a convection oven or air fryer can also do the job.

Regardless of which option you choose, each heat press or oven will have its own set of pros and cons. The heat press that makes the most sense for one crafter may not be the best choice for another. You'll want to make your choice based on which kinds of items you'll make, your budget, and the size of your crafting space.

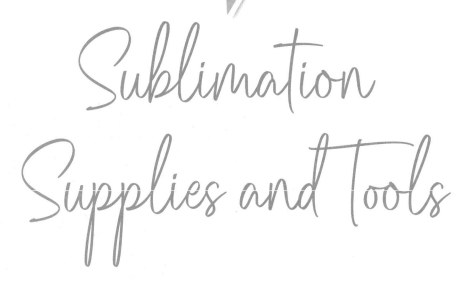

Sublimation Supplies and Tools

In addition to your printer and your heat press, there are a variety of tools and supplies you'll need for sublimation.

We'll start with the things I think are most helpful—my "must-haves"—and then move to the other supplies, tools, and accessories that I think are handy to have as you move into more-advanced projects.

Must-Have Tools & Supplies

Sublimation Paper

Sublimation paper is a must inside your sublimation printer. The paper is designed to hold the ink until it dries and release it effectively when heated so it transfers properly. There are many quality brands of sublimation paper on the market in an assortment of sizes, from standard 8 ½" x 11" (22 x 28 cm) paper to large tabloid 11" x 17" (28 x 43 cm) paper and all the way down to strips of 9" x 4 ½" (23 x 12 cm) paper designed specifically for mugs and other small projects. For this book, I am using Sawgrass TruPix paper and A-Sub paper in a variety of sizes.

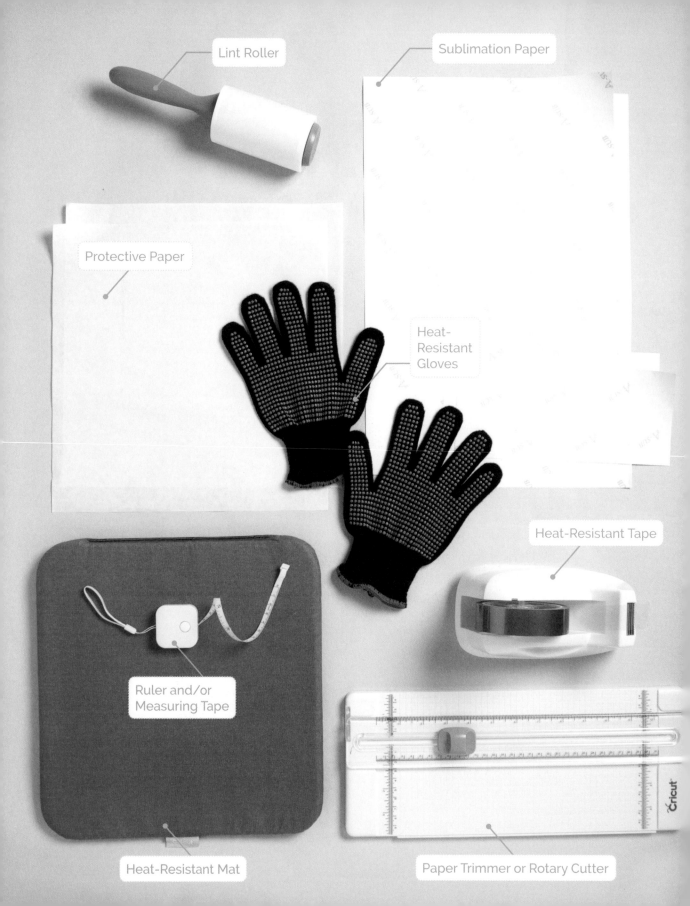

Lint Roller

Sublimation Paper

Protective Paper

Heat-Resistant Gloves

Heat-Resistant Tape

Ruler and/or Measuring Tape

Heat-Resistant Mat

Paper Trimmer or Rotary Cutter

Heat-Resistant Tape

Heat-resistant tape is used to secure your printed sublimation transfer to your blank substrate so that it doesn't shift during pressing. I recommend using blue heat-resistant tape. Many yellow heat-resistant tapes are low quality and might leave a residue or yellow stain on your projects.

Protective Paper

Protective paper is just that: It protects the heat platen of your heat press from ink bleed-through. Bleed-through is when ink from your printed sublimation transfer comes through the paper and deposits where you don't want it.

I prefer unwaxed, uncoated butcher paper. Parchment paper will also work, but it is more expensive. Waxed paper is not a good substitute because the waxy coating can transfer to your substrate or press. I used to use butcher paper on rolls, but now I buy 12" x 12" (31 x 31 cm) sheets (which are actually designed for deli meats!). If you notice any ghosting or ink marks on your protective paper, swap it out for a clean sheet.

A note on Teflon sheets: some crafters use Teflon sheets instead of protective paper, but I don't recommend it. Teflon can trap moisture, which can cause issues with your transfer. Additionally, sublimation ink bleeding through your transfer and onto the Teflon sheet will cause ghost

images on future projects. Finally, the texture of the Teflon sheet may imprint into your substrate in an unappealing way. My recommendation: stick with protective paper instead of using a Teflon sheet.

Lint Roller

Before you press your sublimation project, it's best to run a lint roller over the entire surface of your substrate. Dust, lint, and other small particles can cause spots and other issues with your final image.

Heat-Resistant Gloves

Heat-resistant gloves make it safe and easy to remove projects from a hot press or oven. Using gloves is a lot easier than handling items using pot holders or oven mitts.

Heat-Resistant Mat

Speaking of removing things from a hot press, you'll want to place your hot projects on a heat-resistant mat. The Cricut EasyPress mat is a popular option, but wool pressing mats or silicone mats work as well.

You can see the blowout on this piece of butcher paper. If you don't use butcher paper, that ink around the edges of the image will end up on your press instead.

Polyester Fabric for Testing

I recommend buying several yards of white 100% polyester fabric. This allows you to test your prints before you sublimate them on your substrate. This can save you much trouble and money because you're likely to discover many issues before pressing the image onto your substrate. It's much cheaper to do a test print than to ruin a blank!

Ruler and/or Measuring Tape

To help you align your printed sublimation transfer on your blank substrate, have a measuring tool available. A ruler is good for harder, flat surfaces, whereas a fabric measuring tape is better for soft or curved surfaces.

Paper Trimmer or Rotary Cutter

To cut your printed sublimation transfers down to the size of your project, a paper trimmer can be helpful. I also like using a rotary cutter, acrylic ruler, and self-healing cutting mat for trimming down transfers. This method allows you to cut off the smallest bit of your transfer, which is helpful when you are, for example, trying to trim a transfer to fit perfectly around a tumbler.

Nice-to-Have Tools & Supplies

The following items are helpful to have, but don't feel like you need to invest in everything right away! As you create more with your sublimation printer, you'll figure out which of these things will make your crafting easier.

Rubbing Alcohol and a Microfiber Cloth

A lint roller works for cleaning just about any substrate before applying your printed sublimation transfer, but rubbing alcohol on a microfiber cloth can be more effective on hard substrates like mugs and tumblers. These blanks tend to hold more oils and residues than soft substrates, and the alcohol helps clean the substrate thoroughly. Don't use a cotton ball with the alcohol—the cotton fibers may remain on your blank and can create squiggles and dots in your final image.

Heat Adhesive Spray

Heat adhesive spray can replace heat-resistant tape on many substrates. Just spray a bit of the adhesive on your printed sublimation transfer and press it to your blank. The product is a bit expensive, but it can really speed up the process of preparing a substrate for pressing.

Tape Dispenser

Heat-resistant tape is a must-have, but it can be frustrating and time consuming to cut pieces with scissors. I recommend a tape dispenser. A standard tape dispenser that holds a large roll of tape will work, or you can get an auto-cut tape dispenser that automatically cuts pieces of tape for you when you turn the handle.

Small Fan

If you want to speed up the cooling process a bit (particularly on ceramic projects), a small fan can help cool your projects without cracking or breaking them.

Heat Gun

If you're struggling with overcooking or undercooking your projects (more on this later), you may want to test the actual temperature of your heat press against what the control box says. A heat gun can give you an accurate reading of the temperature of the heat platen. With an accurate measurement of the actual temperature, you can then adjust your heat press temperature setting to compensate accordingly.

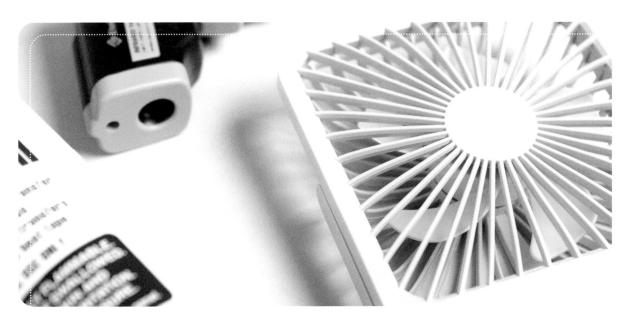

Oven Thermometers

If you're using a convection oven for sublimation, get two oven thermometers—one for each side of your oven. You can use these to check the temperature on each side of the oven. If the heating is uneven, you'll want to rotate your project halfway through to ensure even heating.

Pressing Pillows

Use a pressing pillow for soft blanks and garments with zippers, buttons, seams, and pockets. Place the pillow inside your blank to raise the pressing surface above the troublesome parts of the blank in order to achieve an even press. (For example, the bulkiness of the hood of a hoodie might interfere with you trying to press a design on the hoodie's front. By inserting a pressing pillow, you raise the hoodie's front above the level of the hood.) You can also use other white items (white ensures you won't have any color bleed), such as a folded washcloth, hand towel, or even a cloth diaper. Cotton quilt batting works as well and is easy to trim down to the size you need.

Shrink-Wrap Sleeves

If you want to make projects in a convection oven, shrink-wrap sleeves are your primary option. Because a convection oven doesn't provide the pressure component of a heat press, you need to mimic that pressure on your substrate, which is exactly what a shrink-wrap sleeve does. Shrink-wrap sleeves come in a variety of sizes to fit all sorts of blanks, including tumblers, mugs, dog bowls, and shot glasses.

Silicone Wraps

Silicone wraps are a secondary option for convection oven projects. These are bands of silicone that stretch and secure around a blank to provide the pressure needed for sublimation. Personally, I have found these less successful than shrink-wrap sleeves, but they are inexpensive and reusable, and many crafters prefer them.

Shirt Rulers

If you make T-shirts and other garments, a set of shirt rulers can make lining up your printed sublimation transfer on your blank so much easier. Most come in packs with rulers for various shirt sizes and necklines.

Heat-Conductive Green Pad

Certain substrates like ceramic tiles and ornaments may work better with a heat-conductive rubber pad, also called a green pad. The pad has metal fibers woven into it, meaning it conducts heat really well. The pad protects the substrate from cracking while forming to the shape of the blank to provide an even press. The manufacturer's pressing instructions will let you know if you need one and how to use it. They aren't cheap, so make sure you really need one for the types of projects you want to make. And, if you need one, you need one—there are no viable substitutes.

Nomex Pad

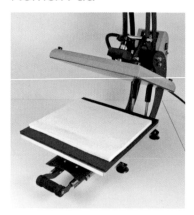

A Nomex pad is a thick piece of heat-resistant felt. It is sometimes used underneath substrates in a heat press to provide cushioning. The manufacturer's instructions for your substrate will tell you if you need to use one. I also use my Nomex pad inside my convection oven on the rack. The rack itself can have hotspots that can show up on a finished project, but the Nomex pad distributes the heat more evenly. You can also use one as a heat-resistant mat as mentioned earlier in this section. As with the heat-conductive green pad, if you need one, you need one—there is no substitute.

Other Items

There are other specific items you may want to have in your craft room, depending on the types of projects you make. For example, you may want a flip-flop assembly tool if you really get into making sublimation flip-flops!

Rubbing Alcohol and a Microfiber Cloth

Shirt Rulers

Nomex Pad

Heat Adhesive Spray

Heat Gun

Oven Thermometers

Small Fan

Heat-Conductive Green Pad

Pressing Pillows

Shrink-Wrap Sleeves

Silicone Wraps

Sublimation Blanks

Blanks are where it really starts to get fun!
There are a ton of options out there. What will
be the first item you create?

You can't sublimate on just any blank substrate. There are two primary features that sublimation blanks need:

- to be made of polyester or to have a poly coating
- to be white or another light color

Let's look at both of these traits in more detail.

POLYESTER AND POLY COATING

For the sublimation process to work, the sublimation ink is turned into a gas, and then the gas needs something to bind with—specifically, polyester or a poly coating.

For soft blanks, this means that sublimation transfers work best on 100% polyester fabric. The lowest you should go is 65% polyester content, but know that the lower the percentage, the more faded your final image may be. You can buy soft blanks labeled specifically for sublimation (which will have a high polyester count), or you can simply buy blanks that have a high polyester count, and sublimation should still work. Soft blanks do not need to be specifically labeled for sublimation—and if they are, you're probably paying extra for that label.

For hard blanks, you need a specialized poly coating for sublimation. This is why you can't take a blank coffee mug from the dollar store and sublimate it. It needs the special poly coating applied to it during manufacturing. When you're shopping for hard blanks, make sure that the blank says it is specifically designed for sublimation.

You cannot sublimate on non-polyester or non-poly-coated blanks without a workaround or compromise, a few of which we'll try in the projects later in this book.

WHITE OR LIGHT COLORS

Sublimation ink is transparent; the color of your substrate will show through. This is why so many substrates are white. White will give you the most vivid and true-to-color transfer. Some sublimation blanks are made using other lighter colors, like gray or a natural canvas color.

Why is this so important? Because if you try to sublimate on a black item or dark garment, your image will be completely invisible, because the black will show through the transparent sublimation ink.

Additionally, if your sublimation image has white in it, your printer will not print the white since sublimation printers don't have white ink. If you're using a blank that is not white, your "white" space on the image will be the color of your blank, not white. We'll talk more about sublimation images in the following section.

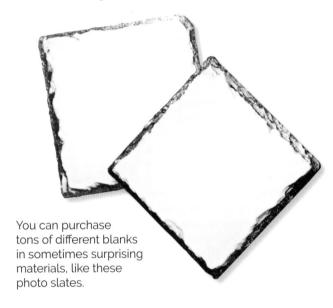

You can purchase tons of different blanks in sometimes surprising materials, like these photo slates.

Sublimation Polyester/Poly-Coating Hacks

As I mentioned before, there are ways to add the poly content needed for sublimation to a variety of substrates. For example, you can use clear or glitter heat-transfer vinyl (HTV) under your sublimation design on cotton or a dark fabric shirt. But unlike with a polyester shirt, the HTV still sits on top of the fabric, meaning you can feel it when you touch it, versus it chemically bonding with the polyester in the shirt itself as in standard sublimation. It will also wash and wear the same as other HTV, which means that over time it may fade, crack, or peel.

There are also poly sprays and coatings to add that poly content to your substrates. I skip them because haven't found one I think works consistently. There is no magic spray in a bottle to make a 100% cotton shirt sublimate exactly like polyester. Sprays, aftermarket coatings, and the like are all a compromise between quality, vibrancy, and longevity, and most do not work well enough to make them worth the cost and effort.

Sublimation Images

Let's talk about the images you're going to use for your sublimation projects! This is where your creativity gets to truly shine.

There was a saying I learned years ago: garbage in = garbage out. In this case, no matter how good your printer is, if you're giving it subpar files to print, you're never going to have a good result.

Most new sublimation crafters start by purchasing files made by other designers, while some may start with designing their own files. Whether you're purchasing files or designing them yourself, you'll want high-quality, high-resolution files to get the best results in your sublimation projects. Of course, this book comes with a free download of all the design files used in the projects in this book—see page 12!

Image Files

FILE TYPES

There are two primary types of images for sublimation crafting: raster and vector. While this may seem technical, having a general knowledge of these two types of images is helpful overall when working with designs for your sublimation projects.

Raster Images

Raster images are PNG, JPG, BMP, GIF, PSD, and TIFF files. These are created in programs that work in pixels, like Photoshop, Affinity Photo, Photoshop Express, Gimp, etc. Photographs are the best example of raster images, but a lot of illustrations work well as raster images too because you can get a lot of detail from the individual pixels.

When a raster image is resized, it loses resolution and becomes pixelated as the image gets larger. This is true of any raster image, so be aware of resizing small images to larger sizes—you'll end up with a pixelated image.

Most purchased sublimation files are created as raster images, though not exclusively.

Vector Images

Vector images are SVG, AI, EPS, and DXF files. These are created in programs that work in vectors, like Adobe Illustrator, Affinity Designer, or Inkscape. A vector image is based on lines and points, not on pixels. This means it can be resized infinitely without losing resolution. Think about fonts, which are also vector-based. You can make a font any size you want, and it never becomes pixelated.

Vector images are often designed for electronic cutting machines, like Cricut and Silhouette, and might not have the same level of detail as raster designs. They are usually solid colors, without grunge textures, watercolor backgrounds, gradients, patterns, or other effects, since those are harder to cut on a cutting machine. That being said, you can print vector images and sublimate them as well.

A crisp (non-pixelated) raster image (left) next to a pixelated raster image (right).

A vector image is infinitely resizable and never becomes pixelated.

FILE FORMATS

Within the two larger categories of raster and vector images are many specific types of image formats. Here are the most-popular ones you'll find for sublimation.

PNG Files

A PNG file, which is raster-based, is the most popular file type for sublimation. PNG files can have a transparent background, making them easy to work with. These files are also "lossless," meaning that when you save your original image as a PNG in a design program, it retains its quality and color, making PNGs ideal for sublimation printing. If you're saving your own designs for printing, a high-resolution PNG is your best bet.

JPG Files

JPG (or JPEG) files are also raster-based, but they were originally created to decrease file size through a process called compression. When you save a file as a JPG, there is some loss in the fidelity/crispness of your image, even when saving as a high-resolution JPG file. The process is irreversible. Once compressed, you will never be able to get those lost pixels back. There are some AI products that attempt to guess and fill in the lost details, but you won't get the exact original image back.

Nevertheless, you will still find JPG files that work as sublimation images. Photographs, for example, are most often saved in a JPG format. And some digital file sellers also sell their images in a JPG format.

Generally, as long as the resolution is high, you can still get a quality sublimation print from a JPG. But if you're struggling with pixelation or it just doesn't look as good as you thought it should, the compression of a JPG could be to blame.

SVG Files

As I mentioned before, SVG files are often designed for cutting machines and are vector-based. If you're going to use an SVG file for sublimation, I suggest saving the file as a high-resolution PNG if possible. Because SVGs are

often built in layers, some printers struggle to handle them properly. Saving as a PNG (where layers are flattened together) allows you to print your image with ease.

Other File Types

You may run across other file types, as mentioned earlier in this section; all will technically work for sublimation if you can print them with your software. More often than not, as a sublimation crafter, you'll be using a PNG, JPG, or SVG file. Yes, you will encounter some folks with more technical ability who use other formats, but you need not follow their lead unless you want to become a professional artwork designer.

FILE RESOLUTION

Resolution applies to raster images, so we're looking at PNG and JPG files when we talk about resolution. A printed image is made up of thousands of tiny dots. The more dots, the higher the resolution. The higher the resolution, the better the print. When purchasing files, you want to make sure they are at least 300 dpi ("dpi" stands for dots per inch). When you're saving files, save them at 300 dpi at the dimensions they are meant to be printed. 300 dpi is the resolution this entire book (and basically every book!) is printed in!

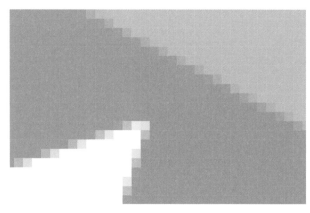

Resolution refers to the number of pixels in an image—like these pixels in the tumbler design (shown on the facing page).

Color: RGB and CMYK

What you see on your screen cannot be 100% accurately represented when printed. This is because your screen's colors are being created with three colors of light (RGB: red, green, and blue), whereas your prints are being made with four colors of ink (CMYK: cyan, magenta, yellow, and black).

The color spectrum on a screen (which is RGB) is much larger than what the four inks in your printer (CMYK) can produce accurately. You can usually get pretty close, but you'll have some inconsistencies, particularly with the luminosity of colors. Some colors, like neon colors, are very difficult to print without specialty inks.

Color in Printed Sublimation Transfers

A printed sublimation transfer will look dull, and the colors may not look accurate before pressing. Trust the process! You can't know for sure if your colors are correct until you press your image to your substrate. This is why I recommend pressing a test print on a 100% polyester piece of fabric. The color is much more vibrant and authentic once your print has been pressed.

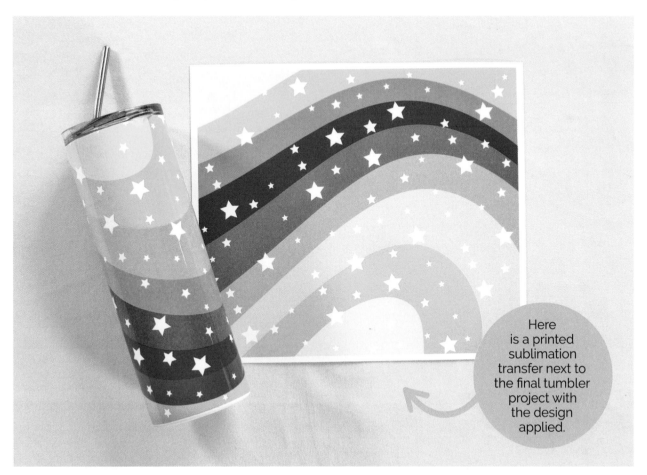

Here is a printed sublimation transfer next to the final tumbler project with the design applied.

Printing Photographs

Sublimating photos can be difficult. Often colors end up oversaturated, and skin tones are often not reproduced well. Always test your photo sublimation prints on a sheet of 100% polyester fabric before using your expensive substrates. You'll want to make sure you have your color dialed in correctly first. Use the tools in your software program to lower the saturation or bring down unwanted colors in your skin tones before printing.

Where to Find Images

Unless you have a background in graphic design, you'll probably start your sublimation journey using files created by other designers. I have a list of sites where you can buy or download free sublimation files at the Sublimation Resources web link on page 4.

Buying from the original designer from a reputable website means you're getting the highest-quality file available. It hasn't been resaved or compressed or badly copied, and it hasn't been stolen and resold at a lower price to undercut the original designer. This is the best way to get sublimation files if you aren't designing them yourself.

Also be aware of copyrighted and licensed images. These images include characters, fonts, and scenes from companies like Disney, Marvel, Harry Potter, and others, as well as things like sports teams or company logos. If you buy copyrighted or licensed images, they are almost always being illegally sold. These companies hold their trademarks very tightly, and you can get into legal trouble for using images with licensed content, even if it's just for personal use. When in doubt, reach out to an attorney familiar with copyright law . . . or just don't use the image in the first place.

While purchasing sublimation designs for your projects is always an option, learning how to use a graphic design software can open up more possibilities in your sublimation crafting.

I love showcasing my vacation photos on metal photo panels!

Modifying Images

There are lots of ways you can take existing designs and make them your own. Here are a few ways you might think about modifying designs:

- Adding text to your image, like a name or a quote
- Layering a background design with text or other sublimation images
- Adding a watercolor, spray paint, or grunge background behind another image
- Scanning photos and adding a sublimation border
- Creating your own pattern with smaller sublimation images
- Adding a monogram
- Layering a photograph with important dates or milestones in text
- Using larger sublimation images for smaller projects
- Making a collage of photos or images

One of the easiest ways to customize is to add letters and words!

SIZING YOUR IMAGE

The easiest way to size your image is to use a ruler or measuring tape to estimate the correct size for your project. For images that have a bleed (where the image runs off the edges of your blank), size your image just a bit larger than your blank. For example, if your coasters are 3 ½" (8.9 cm) wide, size your image at 3 ⅝" (9.2 cm) wide. This will ensure you don't have white space around the edge of your blank.

REVERSING YOUR IMAGE

For almost all sublimation projects, you will need to reverse your image before printing it. This way, when you flip it over and press it to your blank, it will be facing the correct direction. All design software should give you the option to reverse your image, whether on the canvas within the program or within the print settings. This may be called Mirror, Flip, Reverse Page, Emulsion Down, or another similar term.

There are a small number of projects that do not require reversing your image, like the glass cutting board later in this book.

Images in this Book

Get the images used in the projects in this book by going to www.betterdaybooks.com/sublimation-crafting-png-download. You can use these images how I've used them or get creative! For example, use the rainbow pattern on a neoprene laptop sleeve or the "what's the best that could happen" image on a notebook cover; or turn the sublimation patch designs into sublimation stickers; or put the "make waves" image on a polyester swim shirt. Your imagination is the limit!

Sublimation Design Software

To truly unlock your creative potential with sublimation, you'll need to utilize design software to at least some degree.

Software is often one of the most intimidating parts of sublimation, particularly if you don't have any sort of graphic design background. There's no single sublimation software that everyone recommends—it all depends on your needs, skill level, and budget. Sublimation prints can be made using software as simple as Google Docs and as complex as Adobe Photoshop.

For the projects in this book, I am primarily using Sawgrass DesignMate and PrintMate software programs because they integrate seamlessly with my Sawgrass printer. In this section, we'll go through uploading files and using templates, but we won't be doing any graphic design within the software.

If you'd like to use a different program, I have tutorials for using different software programs for sublimation listed at the Sublimation Resources web link on page 4.

Most software programs are updated often, so if my screenshots in this book don't match your software exactly, don't panic. The tools should still be similar, and you can always search online for more information about the processes I use here.

Sawgrass PrintMate Software

PrintMate is a simple, easy-to-use software that allows you to print your sublimation designs directly to your Sawgrass printer without any other software. After the initial download and installation, you don't even need to be connected to the internet.

To use PrintMate, click on the plus sign at the top to start a new project. Make sure you have the correct printer selected if you have more than one Sawgrass printer.

Click "Add Files" and navigate to your file on your computer; it will upload to PrintMate. As you can see, when I first added this Rainbow Tumbler file, I got the message "Image will not fit with current paper size selection."

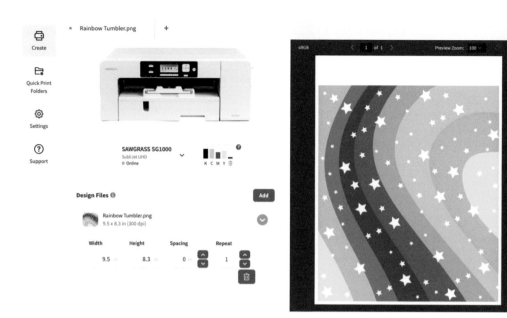

Next, resize your image to fit your blank. For this project, I'm using a 20 oz. (590 mL) skinny tumbler, so I resized my image to be 9.5" (24 cm) wide and 8.3" (21 cm) tall. I will end up trimming this transfer a bit to fit my tumbler exactly, but this size is a good start. See more about resizing your image on page 51.

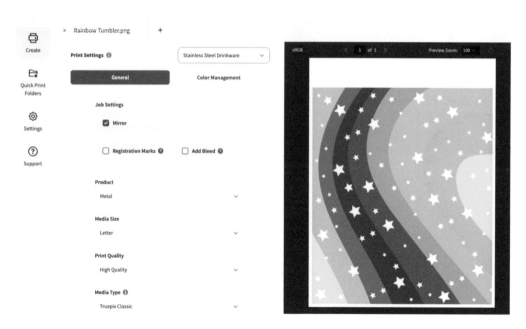

Scroll down to the Print Settings. You can select a preset for different types of substrates, or you can choose your settings manually. For this project, I chose Stainless Steel Drinkware, and it changed my product selection to Metal. When you choose a product, PrintMate will make a calculation for how much ink to lay down on the page for that particular substrate. You can also make other Print Settings selections here, including your paper size, mirroring, or adding a bleed to your print. Remember, for most projects, you will need to mirror your image.

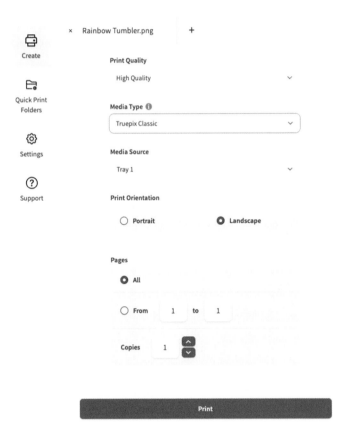

If you continue to scroll down, you can also select your print orientation and how many copies you want to print, among other things.

And that's it! Click "Print," and your project will be sent to the printer.

Sawgrass DesignMate Software

DesignMate is Sawgrass's graphic design software program. While it's a fairly basic design program compared to something more robust like Photoshop, it does have some unique features that make the sublimation printing process a bit easier. This includes using templates, which we'll talk about here. It also has a marketplace component that allows you to list your products for sale if you have a small business.

Templates can make it so much easier to size your images for your projects. For many projects,

you'll just measure the size of your blank and resize your image accordingly. But what if you want, for example, to put an image on both sides of a mug and have the two images spaced equally? That's where templates come in.

When you open DesignMate, you'll start with your product selection. They have a lot of different blanks for you to choose from. If you don't see your blank here, you can click "Custom Canvas" and create your design there. You can also just use PrintMate instead if you're going to be resizing your image without a template.

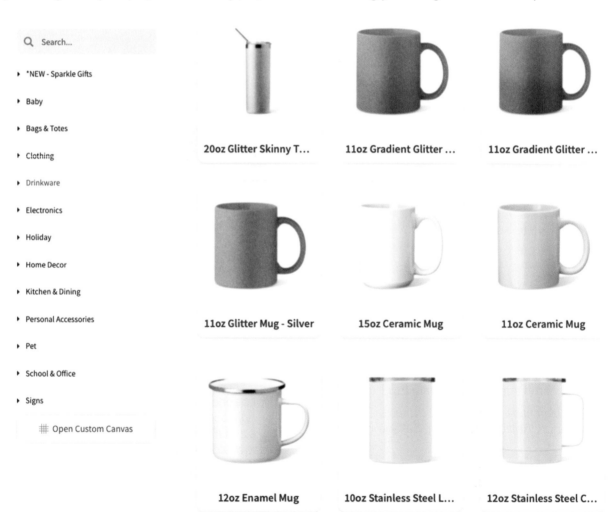

For this project, I chose a 15 oz. (440 mL) ceramic mug from the Drinkware category.

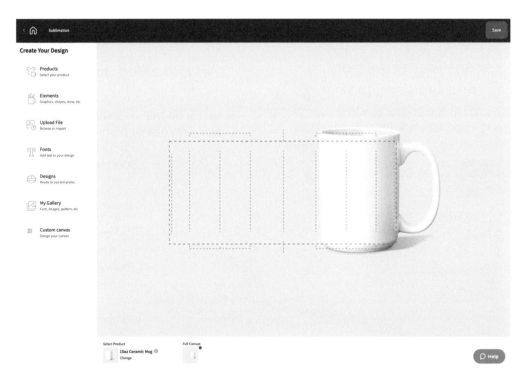

In the design screen, you'll see an image of the mug, plus a template for your image to wrap all the way around the mug with guides for lining up your images.

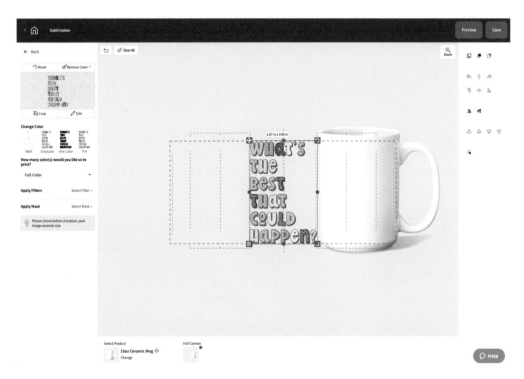

Click "Upload File" to upload your image for your mug, which will appear on the template.

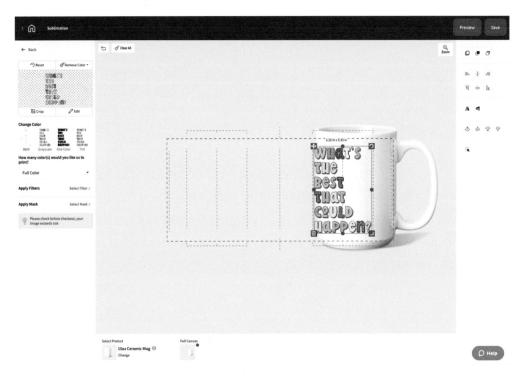

From here, you can use the handle in the bottom right corner to resize your image. Then you can drag and drop it within the guides. Always measure your actual blank to make sure your image is the correct size.

Click "Duplicate" at the upper right to create a second image, and drag and drop it within the guides on the other side of the template.

Next, click "Save" in the upper right. In the next screen, there will be options to set your project for sale using the marketplace. You may or may not want to learn more about this feature, but, either way, you can print your image by clicking "Print" in the upper right.

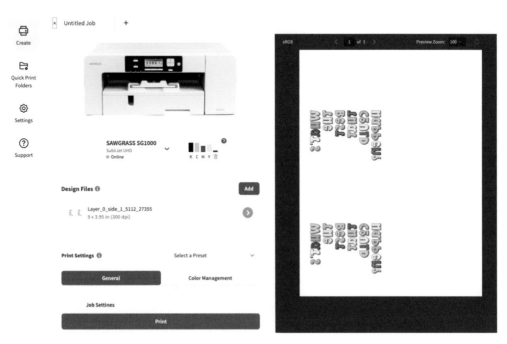

That will open up PrintMate, and you'll follow the PrintMate instructions earlier in this section to print your image.

Learning Graphic Design

If you want to learn more about graphic design in general, I have a few tips no matter what software you are using.

CREATE TIME FOR LEARNING

Set aside a few specific hours a week to specifically learn more about your software. I recommend doing this during the time of the day you're most alert—trying to learn a new software during the sluggish hour after lunch will just make it that much harder! Check out the software developer's website for tutorials, read blogs, or watch YouTube videos.

A lot of times we learn on the fly: "I want to do this specific task for this specific project." While this is not a bad way to learn, it's also helpful to get a stronger grasp of how the software works as a whole so the next time you need a specific task, you'll be able to find what you want to do more easily.

TAKE A CLASS

If you really want to dive in, take a class on your software! Going through a curriculum is often more effective than finding random tutorials online. Classes often have a price tag and time commitment, but I personally find that if I've paid for something, I'm more likely to actually finish it.

JOIN A FACEBOOK GROUP OR FORUM

Many software programs have forums or groups where you can learn from other users. This is helpful if you want to do something specific and can't find a tutorial online to help.

DON'T BE DISCOURAGED

Learning a new software is hard—especially if you aren't particularly tech savvy. Software programs have hundreds (or perhaps thousands) of capabilities, and you don't need to know all of them to design files for sublimation. Don't let it overwhelm you. Take a class or read tutorials to get familiar with the different toolbars and functions. As you learn new things, you'll add them to your design toolbox and you'll find it easier and easier to create the types of designs you want!

Time, Temperature, and Pressure

These three elements are what your heat press uses to finally make the magic happen. In a way, they're the quickest part of any project!

You've got your gear, you've got your image printed, and you're ready to actually set the sublimation process in motion! The next piece of the puzzle is the combination of time, temperature, and pressure in your heat press. These settings are based on your blank substrate. Therefore, pressing a polyester shirt is different than pressing a sublimation photo panel, which is different than pressing a metal water bottle.

The most important thing is to read the manufacturer's instructions carefully before beginning. They should tell you the suggested time, temperature, and pressure for your specific substrate. If you can't locate the manufacturer's instructions, find a similar substrate online and use that as a starting point.

TIME

The press time, also called the dwell time, is the amount of time your heat press is actually pressing your substrate. This can range from as little as 30 seconds to longer than 10 minutes, depending on the item. Always use the countdown feature on your heat press—the last thing you want is to forget your item in the press!

TEMPERATURE

The baseline temperature for sublimation is 360°F–400°F (182°C–205°C), but this will vary for each blank. Wait for your heat press to fully come to temperature before you press your project.

PRESSURE

The pressure refers to the amount of pressure your press is putting on the blank. Most items use medium pressure, but some may use heavy or light pressure.

On many presses, turning the knob (or knobs) on your heat press will increase or decrease the pressure. You'll be able to feel the difficulty or ease of closing the heat press. Light pressure is easy to clamp shut, whereas heavy pressure takes more muscle. Medium pressure is somewhere in between the two.

If you find that you're seeing press marks or tape marks on your final project, try decreasing the pressure just a bit.

Practice Makes Consistent

Getting the perfect press can be a matter of trial and error. Start with the manufacturer's recommended settings and go from there. I have also listed common time, temperature, and pressure settings for each of the projects later in this book.

If you're having issues, I offer suggestions for fixing time, temperature, and pressure settings in the troubleshooting section—see page 76.

As I recommended previously, do a test print and press on a piece of 100% polyester fabric before moving to your blank substrate to make sure your colors and everything else look correct.

Always take notes as you go, making note of time, temperature, pressure, and other considerations. Once you have the perfect combination dialed in, write it down so creating your projects is easier and you'll waste far fewer prints and blanks.

The Sublimation Sandwich

When you're ready to press your project,
you'll need to build a "sublimation sandwich"
that consists of all the necessary layers of
materials for success.

A sublimation sandwich is the stacking order inside your press. You should be able to find the sublimation sandwich stacking order wherever you purchased your blank. I have also included the most common sublimation sandwich diagram for each project in this book. Still refer to the manufacturer's recommendations for your blank—but if you can't find them, the diagrams in this book should help.

Let's look at two different examples to help explain the sandwich.

For the first example, imagine this is the stacking sandwich provided by the manufacturer of a sublimation baby bodysuit:

HEAT SOURCE
PROTECTIVE PAPER
TRANSFER FACE DOWN
BLANK BODYSUIT FACE UP
PROTECTIVE PAPER
PRESSING PILLOW
PROTECTIVE PAPER
PRESSING PAD
BOTTOM SURFACE

- First, place a sheet of protective paper on the bottom pad of the heat press to protect it from any ink bleed-through.
- Then add the baby bodysuit. To prevent bleed-through, put a pressing pillow and an additional sheet of protective paper between the two layers of the bodysuit. Smooth out any wrinkles.
- Next comes the printed sublimation transfer. Tear around the transfer instead of cutting it to reduce any press marks (this is a good trick for soft blanks), and use heat-resistant tape to adhere it to the bodysuit face down.
- Then add another sheet of protective paper to protect the top platen of the heat press.

Now you're ready to press your baby bodysuit according to the time, temperature, and pressure recommendations of the manufacturer.

Next, let's look at the stacking sandwich for a mug inside a mug press. This is a bit different because you are wrapping your transfer and protective elements around your mug instead of laying everything flat in a stack.

- First, we have the mug with the printed sublimation transfer secured to the outside of the mug with heat-resistant tape.
- Then there are two layers of protective paper to protect the press.

And that's it—this mug is ready to press according to the manufacturer's time, temperature, and pressure recommendations.

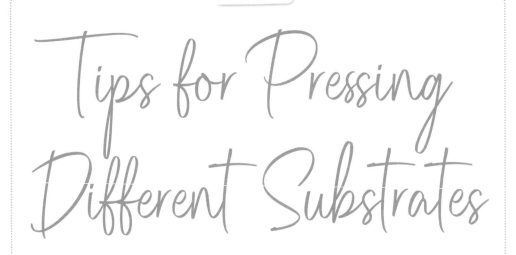

Tips for Pressing Different Substrates

Not every substrate is alike! Depending on what you're pressing, there are different ways to make the process easier, cleaner, and more successful.

It's finally time to press your project! Press down on the handle of your heat press to press your project and start the timer.

When the timer beeps, carefully open the heat press and allow your project to cool for a few minutes. However, if you're using a press where the project is still touching the heating element (like a mug press or a tumbler press), remove the blank from the press right away.

Allow the project to cool to the touch before removing the transfer. This will help prevent ghosting or blurred images. You may notice some yellowing of the transfer or protective paper after your press—this is totally normal.

Generally, one press is sufficient for most projects. But there are some cases where you will want to double-press. For example, if you're making a full-coverage tumbler in a tumbler press, you'll want to press once, rotate the tumbler to get even pressing all the way around, and press again. We'll talk about some double-pressed projects later in the book.

Now let's look at the most-popular substrates and different tips and tricks for getting the best results with each.

APPAREL AND OTHER SOFT BLANKS

Clothing, pillowcases, aprons, bags, bandannas, flags, and more.

- Use a lint roller to clean your fabric before pressing. This will help you avoid spots on your image and fabric after pressing.

- Pre-press your blanks for 15 seconds. Pre-pressing your blanks removes wrinkles and moisture and gives you a perfectly flat surface for your transfer.

- Use heat-resistant tape or heat-resistant spray to secure your image to the substrate before pressing so it won't shift while in the heat press.

- Keep your polyester count high. As I mentioned previously, sublimation transfers need polyester fabric to bond with the ink. Use 65% polyester and above—the higher the polyester count, the more even and vibrant your image will be.

- "Deckle" the edge of your transfer. If you notice a harsh paper line around your design after pressing, try ripping the paper around your image so the edges are not straight. This can help decrease unsightly pressing lines.

- Use a pressing pillow on garments with zippers, buttons, seams, and pockets to help get an even press.

CERAMIC, SANDSTONE, AND PORCELAIN

Mugs, coasters, tumblers, ornaments, plates, tiles, and more.

- Wipe down your blank with alcohol to clean it before pressing—this will help you avoid spots and oil marks on your substrate after pressing.

- Peel back any clear protective film on top of your blank. This can be hard to see on some blanks, so check carefully.

- Use heat-resistant tape or heat-resistant spray to secure your image to the substrate before pressing so it won't shift while in the heat press.

- Sublimate the correct side. The correct side is obvious when you're doing some blanks (like mugs), but a ceramic tile or coaster will most likely have a very white side and an off-white side. You want to sublimate your image to the whitest side, which is the side that has the sublimation coating.

- Pay attention to the stacking sandwich—some ceramic blanks are pressed upside down according to the manufacturer's instructions. The blank will face away from the heating element of your heat press with the image below it, so you're heating it from the back through to the front.

- The manufacturer's instructions may have you use a specialized pad (for example, a green rubber pad or a Nomex pad) with your blank to ensure an even press without breaking your substrate. If you're using a specialized pad, the press time will likely increase, so read the manufacturer's instructions carefully.

- While all blanks come out of the press very hot, be aware that ceramic blanks remain hot a lot longer than many other blanks.

NEOPRENE

Can koozies, coasters, laptop sleeves, bags, wristlets, mouse pads, and more.

• While good ventilation is recommended for all sublimation processes, it is especially recommended for neoprene, which has a particularly rubbery smell. If possible, open a window, turn on a fan, and run an air purifier. Wearing a respirator mask can help.

• Use a lint roller to clean your neoprene before pressing—this will help you avoid spots on your image after pressing.

• Many neoprene blanks have two sides that you will want to sublimate (like can koozies and bags). Sublimate one side at a time.

• Heat-resistant tape doesn't stick well to neoprene, so try a heat-resistant adhesive spray instead.

• Once you've removed your project from the heat press, place it under a book or other heavy object to prevent curling.

METAL

Tumblers, key chains, photo panels, badges, frames, mugs, and more.

- Peel back any clear protective film on top of your blank. This can be hard to see on some blanks, so check carefully. If in doubt, use a weeding hook to gently check around the edges.

- Metal can get a bit spotty if there's any lint or dust, so clean your blank well with rubbing alcohol before adding your printed sublimation transfer.

- Heat-resistant spray can leave marks on stainless steel, so heat-resistant tape is a better option.

- The manufacturer's instructions may have you use a specialized pad (for example, a green rubber pad or a Nomex pad) with your blank to ensure an even press. If you're using a specialized pad, the press time will likely increase, so read the manufacturer's instructions carefully.

- While all blanks come out of the press very hot, be aware that thick metal blanks remain hot a lot longer.

OTHER BLANKS

There are so many blanks out there to test and try! Visit the Sublimation Resources web link on page 4 for where to search out and buy a huge variety of sublimation substrates.

Cheat Sheet Recap

There was a lot of info in the previous section! All the detail included up to this point is valuable—which is why I included it!—but it's important to remember that sublimation crafting is, in essence, a series of achievable steps that you take one by one until you're holding a super-cool finished project in your hands. Here's a quick recap of the sublimation process from start to finish.

CHOOSE A PROJECT/BLANK

What do you want to make? Get your hands on the right polyester or poly-coated blank!

CHOOSE YOUR PRINTER

Purchase, turn on, or set up your chosen printer, whether it's one you've converted or a sublimation-specific printer.

3

CHOOSE YOUR HEAT PRESS

Make sure you have the right heat press for the type of project you're making.

4

GATHER YOUR TOOLS

Review how you'll press your chosen project and make sure you have each of the necessary tools, such as heat-resistant tape, heat-resistant gloves, etc. (If you're making one of the projects featured in this book, you can simply refer to the supplies list!)

5

PREPARE AND PRINT YOUR IMAGE

What fun design will you be sublimating onto your blank? Purchase or design the image file, customize it if desired, and print it out on sublimation paper.

6

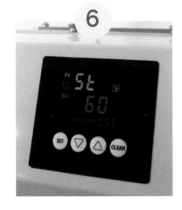

PREPARE TO PRESS

Figure out the best time, temperature, and pressure for your particular substrate. Review the manufacturer's instructions, the project instructions (if applicable), and the different substrate tips in the previous section so that you're completely ready to go.

7

PRESS YOUR PROJECT!

Assemble your sublimation sandwich and get pressing! After all that prep work, you'll be holding your finished object in your hands in a matter of minutes.

Troubleshooting

You've read and followed all the instructions in this book and still something goes wrong with your sublimation transfer? We've all been there!

Here are some of the most common problems you'll run into, as well as steps to fix them. Reading this section ahead of time will give you a leg up when you start sublimating your first few blanks.

THE SUBLIMATION TRANSFER HAS STREAKS OR BANDING

If you notice that you can see the printer lines in your printed image, or if you have white or miscolored streaks in your print, there are several things that may have gone wrong that you can try to fix. See an example of this issue below.

Print Quality Is Low

Ensure you have the highest-quality print setting turned on. When a printer is in normal or ink-saving mode, you are much more likely to see printer banding.

Bidirectional Printing Is Turned On

Turn off bidirectional printing. Bidirectional printing means the print head prints in both directions from left to right and then right to left. This increases the print speed but may reduce vertical alignment, causing banding.

Printer Heads Are Clogged

Additionally, streaks or bands may appear on a printed image due to clogged printer head nozzles, especially if it has been a while since you've printed anything. Run a printer head nozzle check, print purge files, and perform one or more cleanings to clear the print heads. If you are using an Epson printer, use "Power Clean" only as a last result. Wait 12–24 hours after a major cleaning cycle runs to let air work its way out of the printer's ink feed lines.

THE SUBLIMATION TRANSFER IS FADED

It's no fun to peel back the sublimation paper to reveal a faded image. Here are a few explanations for what may have caused the fading and what you can do to ensure a bright, even image.

Low-Quality Paper

Make sure you're using a high-quality sublimation paper. You'll also want to be sure you're printing on the correct (generally the whitest and brightest) side of your sublimation paper. Most sublimation paper has a watermark on the back—ensure you're printing on the front.

Substrate Issues

You'll also get a faded image if you're not using a polyester or poly-coated substrate, as mentioned previously. Additionally, low-quality blanks may give poor results. Substrates with slightly uneven surfaces may benefit from being pressed with a heat-conductive green pad.

Not Enough Heat Press Pressure

Another common problem is not enough pressure with your press. Without the firm pressure of the heat press, the sublimation ink dissipates into the air instead of being pressed into the surface of your blank.

THE SUBLIMATION TRANSFER IS BLURRY

If your image looks blurry or text and images are not as sharp as they look on your printed transfer, you could have one of several problems.

Not Enough Tape

Be sure everything is taped as tightly as possible. If your transfer shifts or lifts at all, it can cause a blurry image. When in doubt, use more tape.

Too Much Heat or Time

If your image looks blurry when you pull the transfer paper off, you may have applied too much heat or pressed for too long, causing your image to bleed out a bit. Often, reducing your press time will resolve the issue.

Uneven Pressure

If you find that only parts of your image are blurred, you may have uneven heat press pressure. If there are any gaps in your pressure, your image may "gas out," which means the ink sucks into the gap as it turns into a gas. This can cause blurring in your image. To fix this, make sure that the platen of your heat press or mug press has even pressure across your whole image. To do this, make sure your blank is as flat or straight in the press as possible, and, if you can adjust pressure areas separately (like with a tumbler press), make sure the pressure screws are evenly rotated.

Air Gaps

If your image is not flat against the surface of your blank, it can cause blurry areas on your blank. For example, it's very hard to get a flat surface (paper) to be perfectly flat against a curved edge (like the bottom of a tumbler), so often you'll see blurriness in cases like this.

If you are struggling with blurred edges on projects like the tumbler shown below, trim your transfer so it doesn't wrap all the way around the bottom curve, leaving a small amount of white space instead. The result (shown at bottom) is much cleaner.

Moisture Issues

Finally, you may have an issue with moisture, especially if you live in a humid climate. Let your substrate sit under your heat press with it open, just hovering over your substrate—not clamped down—for 15 seconds or so. This will help dry your substrate so you'll have a cleaner press. In the photo below, you can see a clean transfer compared to a transfer where there was too much moisture, resulting in a faded final product.

You may also find moisture in your sublimation paper itself. Keep your paper in a dark cabinet in the box it came in until you're ready to use it. Then print your image and transfer it right away so it doesn't have time to absorb any moisture from the air.

If you live in a very humid climate or do not have central air-conditioning, you may find it helpful to place a dehumidifier in your craft room.

THE SUBLIMATION TRANSFER HAS SPOTS

Sometimes you'll notice tiny dots, spots, or squiggles on your project. There's one likely culprit.

Dust and Lint

Most likely, dots and spots are due to dust or lint that made its way onto your substrate or printed transfer image. The high heat of your press can sublimate the color of the lint onto your substrate!

For soft fabrics, use a lint roller before you press. For hard surfaces, wipe clean with alcohol and a lint-free cloth.

THE SUBLIMATION TRANSFER GHOSTED

If you notice a ghosted double image of your transfer or your image, you're probably dealing with one main problem.

Shifting Transfer

Sometimes your image may shift while you're pressing it. This primarily happens when you open or close your heat press. Try opening and closing your heat press slowly, and use heat-resistant tape or heat-resistant adhesive spray to adhere your printed image to your blank. In the photo below, you can see how extreme ghosting can look.

THE SUBLIMATION TRANSFER COLOR IS OFF

This is a big one, and I know it's a huge headache for a lot of sublimation crafters using a converted printer. You have this beautiful image on your computer, but when you transfer it to your substrate, your color is totally off. What may have happened?

No ICC Profile

The main problem is that you probably don't have an ICC profile selected in your design software. This can be the key to getting the correct color in your images if you're using a converted printer like an Epson. Visit the Sublimation Resources web link on page 4 for more information on ICC profiles in converted printers.

Sublimation-specific printers, however, will do their color correction within the printer, so you shouldn't have to worry about installing an ICC profile.

Monitor Color versus Printer Color

As I mentioned previously, your printer may have trouble rendering some images exactly like you see them on your computer screen. This is because the colors on your screen are made up of three colors of pixels made of light (RGB), but your printer uses four physical inks (CMYK). There are just some colors that your printer can't render properly using ink, such as neon colors. If you'd like to read more on this, search online for "CMYK gamut versus RGB."

Overcooked or Undercooked

Does your black ink look brown? That could mean you overheated your item and cooked it too long. Does it look dull or faded or green? You may have undercooked your item. Try adjusting your time settings to see if you can get your blanks to be true to color.

THE SUBLIMATION TRANSFER IS BACKWARD

This one is pretty self-explanatory, and can be a truly unpleasant surprise when there's text involved!

Double-Reversed or Unreserved Image

We talked previously about how you need to reverse your image before printing so it will appear the right way when you transfer it to your substrate. That being said, it's pretty easy to forget to mirror or to accidentally double-mirror your image.

For example, there are two places in Photoshop to reverse an image. The first is in the Photoshop printer settings and is labeled "Emulsion Down." The second is in the printer settings and is labeled "Mirror Image." If you have both these settings checked, they cancel each other out. The answer here is to check only one of those boxes and to confirm that your printout is reversed. If it's readable when you print it out, go back and mirror your image and print again.

SHRINK-WRAP HAS STUCK TO YOUR PROJECT

There are two primary possibilities for what went wrong here.

Your Project Cooled

It's so much easier to remove shrink-wrap from a project while it's still warm. Wear heat-resistant gloves and peel back the shrink-wrap right after your project has come out of the oven. If needed, you can reheat your shrink-wrap with a heat gun, but don't make it so hot that it may sublimate your image again.

Low-Quality Shrink-Wrap

There's also a chance you're using a low-quality shrink-wrap. If possible, purchase your shrink-wrap from a sublimation distributor (see a list at the Sublimation Resources web link on page 4) instead of an online marketplace like Amazon. Yes, quality shrink-wrap may cost a bit more, but it won't ruin your blank like cheap shrink-wrap can.

PART 2

Let's Make Stuff!

For all the following projects, I share the time, temperature, and pressure settings that are common for the substrates being used, as well as a suggested sublimation sandwich. As always, I recommend checking the manufacturer's recommended settings for your particular substrate before pressing.

T-shirt

A T-shirt is the perfect first project because the process is straightforward. You can apply this process to other apparel as well, including hoodies, baby bodysuits, aprons, and more. This project will help you become familiar with the sublimation sandwich as well as with using a heat press.

TOOLS & MATERIALS

- Sublimation paper
- Sublimation T-shirt
- Lint roller
- Pressing pillow
- Heat-resistant tape
- Protective paper
- Heat press
- Heat-resistant gloves

RECOMMENDED SETTINGS

- Pre-press time: 15 seconds
- Press time: 45–60 seconds
- Temperature: 385°F (195°C)
- Pressure: medium

SUBLIMATION SANDWICH

This diagram shows the order of the layers for pressing your project. Refer to this visual if you need to as you follow the step-by-step instructions!

BEFORE YOU BEGIN

- A T-shirt ruler can be very helpful when placing your transfer on your shirt. Using a ruler is usually more accurate than eyeballing it.

INSTRUCTIONS

1. Upload your image to your software and resize to fit your shirt.

2. Print your transfer, making sure to reverse your image before printing.

3. Set your heat press time and temperature.

4. Lint-roll your shirt to remove any debris.

5. Position your shirt on the bottom of your heat press plate.

6. Smooth out the shirt so it's wrinkle-free and pre-press the shirt for 15 seconds to remove any moisture. Let cool for a bit, then remove the shirt from the press.

7. Slide a pressing pillow and a sheet of protective paper between the two layers of your shirt to raise the pressing surface and prevent bleed-through.

8. Tear around the edge of your printed sublimation transfer instead of cutting with scissors. This helps reduce pressing marks on your shirt.

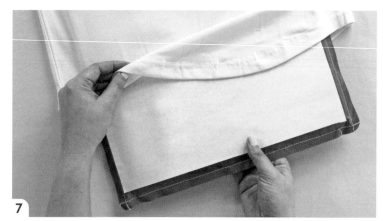

10

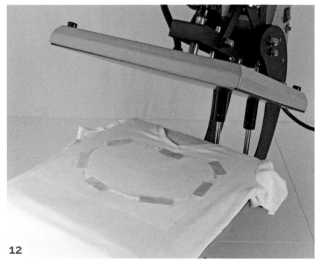

12

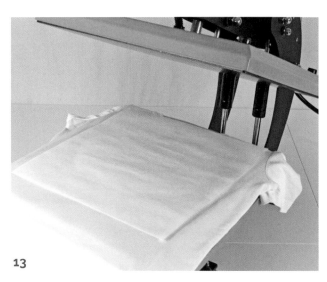

13

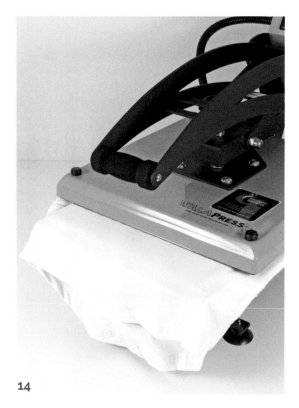

14

9. Place your transfer face down on your shirt. Use a T-shirt ruler or measuring tape to make sure it is centered.

10. Use heat-resistant tape to secure your transfer to the shirt.

11. Place a sheet of protective paper on the bottom pad of your heat press.

12. Position your shirt (with the protective paper and pressing pillow) on the protective paper.

13. Place a sheet of protective paper on top of the transfer.

14. Press your shirt for the recommended time.

15. Carefully open the press and allow your shirt to cool for a bit before removing it. Remove the protective paper and transfer to reveal your finished T-shirt.

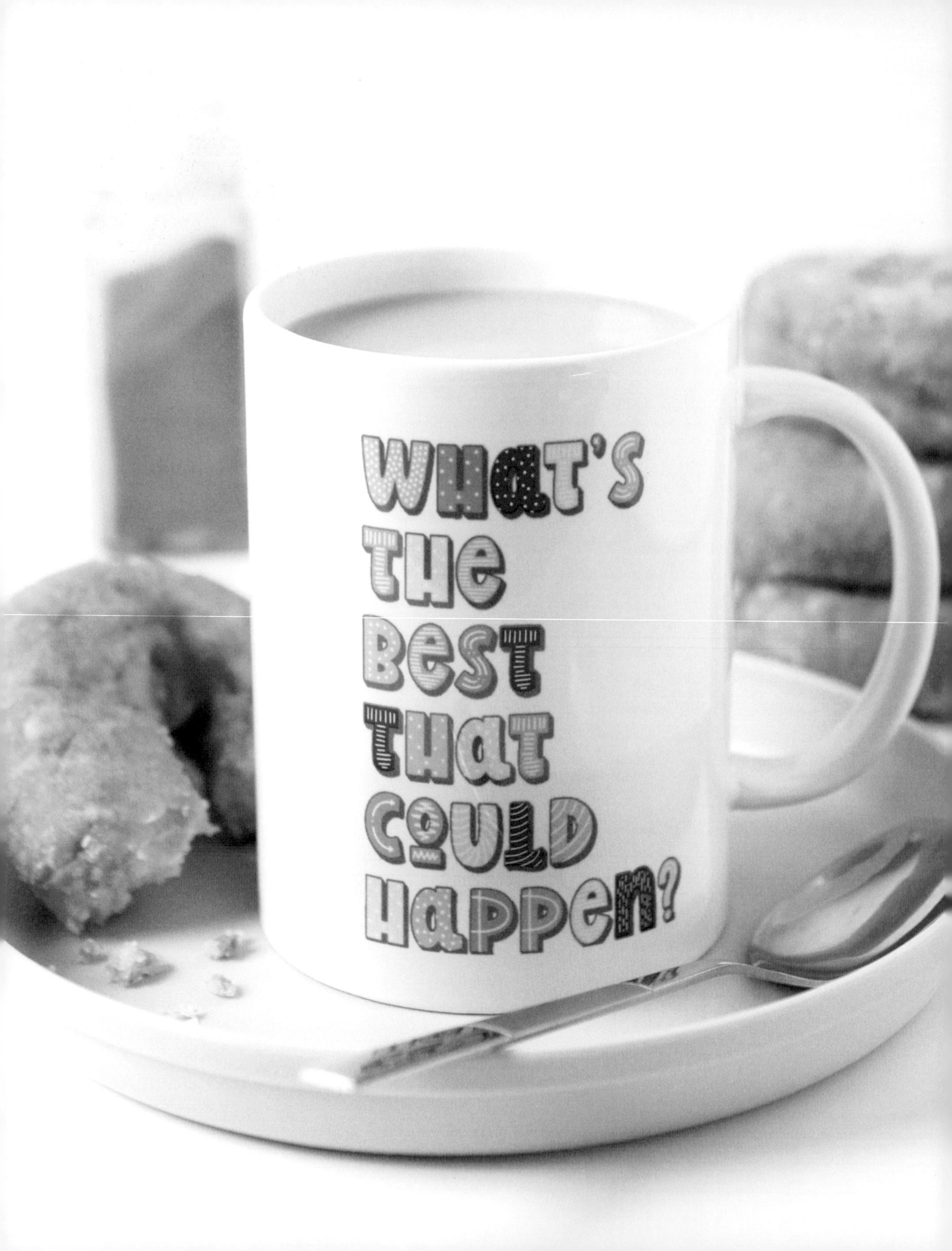
WHAT'S
THE
BEST
THAT
COULD
HAPPEN?

Mug

Mugs make great gifts! Fill your sublimated mug gift with all sorts of goodies, like yummy sweets, a pair of cozy socks, or the ingredients for hot chocolate. I'm using a mug press to make my mug, but you can also use the convection oven method that is used with the tapered tumbler (see page 128).

TOOLS & MATERIALS

- Sublimation paper
- Sublimation mug
- Lint roller, or alcohol and microfiber cloth
- Paper trimmer, or rotary cutter with acrylic ruler and self-healing cutting mat
- Heat-resistant tape
- Protective paper
- Mug press
- Heat-resistant gloves
- Heat-resistant mat

RECOMMENDED SETTINGS

- Press time: 4 minutes
- Temperature: 400˚F (205˚C)
- Pressure: medium

SUBLIMATION SANDWICH

This diagram shows the order of the layers for pressing your project. Refer to this visual if you need to as you follow the step-by-step instructions!

BEFORE YOU BEGIN

- To waste less paper, use mug-sized sublimation paper.

- If possible, use a mug template within your design software. A template is particularly helpful for getting your images centered on both sides of the mug.

- Ceramic stays hot much longer than other materials. Use heat-resistant gloves if you want to remove your transfer from your mug before it has fully cooled.

- Do not wash your sublimated mug on sanitize mode in the dishwasher. The high temperatures can re-sublimate and fade the ink.

INSTRUCTIONS

1. Upload your image to your software and resize to fit your mug. Duplicate the image for the other side of your mug if desired.

2. Print your transfer, making sure to reverse your image before printing.

3. Turn on your mug press. Set your time and temperature if your mug press requires it.

4. Lint-roll your mug or use alcohol and a microfiber cloth to clean it.

5. Trim your printed sublimation transfer to fit your mug. Make sure your image will be at least ½" (1.3 cm) away from the handle. Most mug presses cannot press close to the handle.

6. Wrap your transfer around your mug as tightly as possible and secure with heat-resistant tape. If your design goes all the way to the top and bottom of your mug, tape around the top and bottom as well.

7. Wrap two sheets of protective paper tightly around your mug and secure with heat-resistant tape.

8. Press your mug for the recommended time.

9. Wearing your heat-resistant gloves, carefully open the mug press, remove the mug, and set it on a heat-resistant surface.

10. Wait for the mug to cool for a bit, then remove the protective paper and transfer to see your final mug design.

Skinny Tumbler

Tumblers are one of the most popular sublimation crafts, but it can be difficult to avoid seam marks and blurry edges at the top and bottom if you don't tape your project properly. For this project, I'm using a 20 oz. (600 mL) skinny tumbler in a tumbler press, but you can also use the convection oven method that is used with the tapered tumbler (see page 128).

TOOLS & MATERIALS

- Sublimation paper
- Sublimation tumbler
- Lint roller, or alcohol and microfiber cloth
- Paper trimmer, or rotary cutter with acrylic ruler and self-healing cutting mat
- Heat-resistant tape
- Protective paper
- Tumbler press
- Heat-resistant gloves
- Heat-resistant mat

RECOMMENDED SETTINGS

- Press time: 2 minutes; rotate halfway through
- Temperature: 375°F (190°C)
- Pressure: medium

SUBLIMATION SANDWICH

This diagram shows the order of the layers for pressing your project. Refer to this visual if you need to as you follow the step-by-step instructions!

BLANK TUMBLER
TRANSFER FACE IN
PROTECTIVE PAPER
HEAT SOURCE

BEFORE YOU BEGIN

- Remove the lid and the straw before sublimating the tumbler.

- Using a rotary cutter with an acrylic ruler and self-healing cutting mat is the best way to trim your transfer because you can cut off the narrowest strips of your transfer. You want the transfer to wrap around your tumbler so the edges overlap ever so slightly. That way you don't have a white seam down the side of the tumbler. If you trim it too small, reprint and retrim your transfer.

- If you are struggling with blurriness at the bottom in particular, trim your transfer so it doesn't wrap all the way around the bottom curve, leaving a small amount of white space. See the photo on page 78 for what this looks like.

- Tape is your best friend when it comes to minimizing seams and blurriness at the top and bottom of your tumbler. More is usually better.

- Do not wash your sublimated tumbler in the dishwasher. The dishwasher can ruin the vacuum sealing on the tumbler.

INSTRUCTIONS

1. Upload your image to your software and resize to fit your tumbler.

2. Print your transfer, making sure to reverse your image before printing.

3. Set your tumbler press time and temperature.

4. Lint-roll your tumbler or use alcohol and a microfiber cloth to clean it.

5. Trim your printed sublimation transfer to fit your tumbler.

6. Wrap your transfer around your tumbler as tightly as possible and secure the seam with strips of heat-resistant tape.

7. Tape the top and bottom of the tumbler, using your thumbs to really press the transfer onto the curved edges of the tumbler.

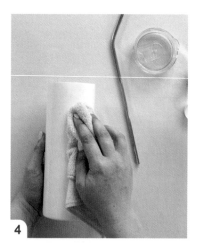

4

5

6

7

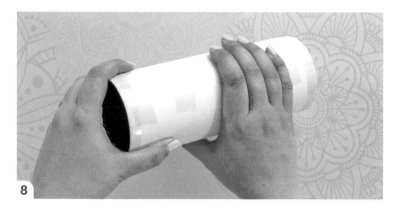

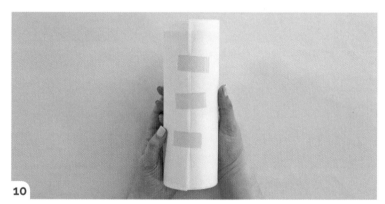

8. Roll the top and bottom edges of the tumbler on a table or self-healing cutting mat to press the transfer onto the tumbler. You want the transfer to "hug" the curve of the tumbler at the top and bottom with no gaps.

9. Add a long piece of tape along the seam of your transfer. Run your thumbnail along the seam to press the tape into the seam and minimize potential blowout.

10. Wrap two sheets of protective paper tightly around your tumbler and secure with heat-resistant tape.

11. Press your tumbler for the recommended time. Wearing your heat-resistant gloves, rotate the tumbler halfway through the pressing time.

12. After the full pressing time is up, wearing your heat-resistant gloves, carefully open the tumbler press, remove the tumbler, and set it on a heat-resistant surface.

13. Wait a few minutes for the tumbler to cool, then remove the transfer to reveal your image.

14. Add your lid and your straw, and you have a ready-to use tumbler.

Neoprene Mouse Pad

A mouse pad is another easier project that is good for beginners. Use patterns, individual designs, or even photos to customize your project. Making a mouse pad will help set you up for other neoprene projects such as koozies and laptop sleeves.

TOOLS & MATERIALS

- Sublimation paper
- Sublimation mouse pad
- Lint roller
- Heat-resistant tape
- Protective paper
- Heat press
- Heat-resistant gloves
- Heat-resistant mat

RECOMMENDED SETTINGS

- Press time: 75–90 seconds
- Temperature: 400˚F (205˚C)
- Pressure: light to medium

SUBLIMATION SANDWICH

This diagram shows the order of the layers for pressing your project.
Refer to this visual if you need to as you follow the step-by-step instructions!

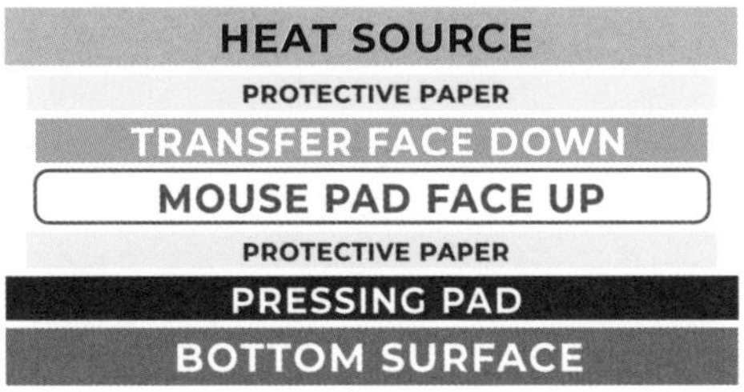

HEAT SOURCE

PROTECTIVE PAPER

TRANSFER FACE DOWN

MOUSE PAD FACE UP

PROTECTIVE PAPER

PRESSING PAD

BOTTOM SURFACE

BEFORE YOU BEGIN

- Neoprene can have a particularly off-putting smell, so make sure you are working in a well-ventilated area.

- After pressing, place something heavy, such as a stack of books, on top of your mouse pad to prevent it from warping.

INSTRUCTIONS

1. Upload your image to your software and resize to fit your mouse pad.

2. Print your transfer, making sure to reverse your image before printing.

3. Set your heat press time and temperature.

4. Lint-roll your mouse pad to remove any debris.

5. Trim your transfer to fit your mouse pad.

6. Tape your transfer to your mouse pad using heat-resistant tape.

7. Place a sheet of protective paper on the bottom pad of your heat press.

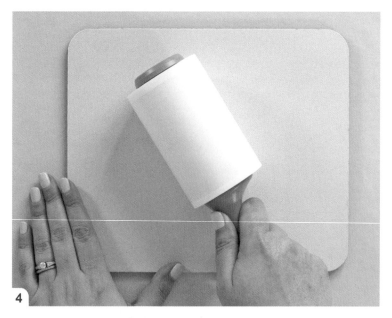

8. Position your mouse pad on the protective paper with the mouse pad facing up and the transfer facing down.

9. Place a sheet of protective paper on top of the transfer.

10. Press your mouse pad for the recommended time.

11. Wearing your heat-resistant gloves, open the press, remove the mouse pad, and set it on a heat-resistant surface. Place something heavy on top of the mouse pad while it cools to prevent warping.

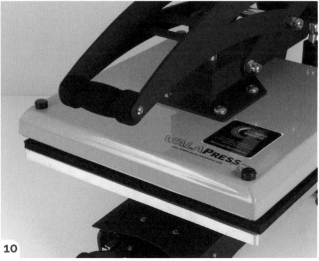

Wine Bag

"Sip" back and relax with this cute wine bag! Projects like this are simple to make and fun to customize for your favorite host or hostess. This is also a gift that can be reused in the future for more bottles of bubbly!

TOOLS & MATERIALS

- Sublimation paper
- Sublimation wine bag
- Lint roller
- Pressing pillow
- Heat-resistant tape
- Protective paper
- Heat press
- Heat-resistant gloves

RECOMMENDED SETTINGS

- Pre-press time: 15 seconds
- Press time: 60 seconds
- Temperature: 385˚F (195˚C)
- Pressure: medium

SUBLIMATION SANDWICH

This diagram shows the order of the layers for pressing your project. Refer to this visual if you need to as you follow the step-by-step instructions!

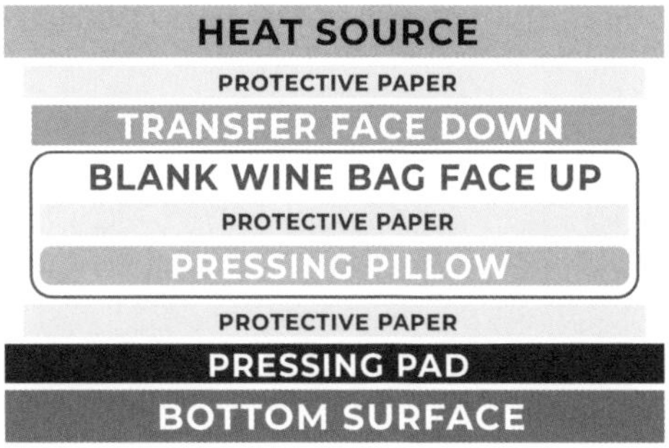

HEAT SOURCE
PROTECTIVE PAPER
TRANSFER FACE DOWN
BLANK WINE BAG FACE UP
PROTECTIVE PAPER
PRESSING PILLOW
PROTECTIVE PAPER
PRESSING PAD
BOTTOM SURFACE

BEFORE YOU BEGIN

- When placing your image on your wine bag, shift it toward the top of the bag a bit instead of centering it. That way, when there is a bottle of wine in the bag, the design won't end up underneath the bottom of the bottle.

- Most pressing pillows are too large for a wine bag, so try a folded washcloth or hand towel or a folded piece of cotton batting instead.

INSTRUCTIONS

1. Upload your image to your software and resize to fit your wine bag.

2. Print your transfer, making sure to reverse your image before printing.

3. Set your heat press time and temperature.

4. Lint-roll your wine bag to remove any debris.

5. Position your wine bag on the bottom of your heat press plate.

6. Smooth out the wine bag so it's wrinkle-free and pre-press your wine bag for 15 seconds to remove any moisture. Let cool for a bit, then remove the wine bag from the press.

7. Use a washcloth, folded towel, or piece of cotton batting plus a piece of protective paper between the two layers of your wine bag to raise the pressing surface and prevent bleed-through.

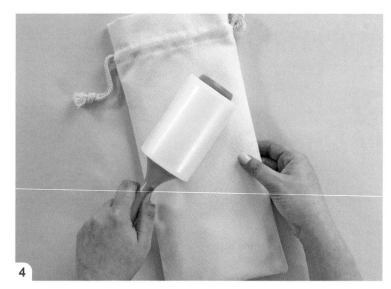

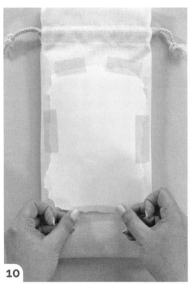

8

10

8. Tear around the edge of your printed sublimation transfer instead of cutting with scissors. This helps reduce pressing marks on your wine bag.

9. Place your sublimation transfer face down on your wine bag, making sure it's centered (see note in Before You Begin).

10. Use heat-resistant tape to secure your transfer to the wine bag.

11. Place a piece of protective paper on the bottom pad of your heat press.

12. Position your wine bag (with the protective paper and pressing pillow) on the protective paper.

13. Place a sheet of protective paper on top of the transfer.

14. Press your wine bag for the recommended time.

15. Carefully open the press and allow your wine bag to cool for a bit. Remove the protective paper and transfer to reveal your finished wine bag.

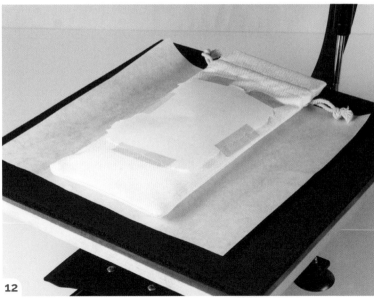

12

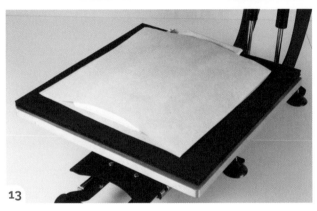

13

14

Ceramic Coasters

Pair the wine bag with this set of coasters to make a great gift for your favorite drinks lover! In this project, you'll learn how to press multiple blanks at once. This process works well for all sorts of smaller blanks such as ornaments, earrings, key chains, and more.

TOOLS & MATERIALS

- Sublimation paper
- Ceramic sublimation coasters
- Lint roller, or alcohol and microfiber cloth
- Heat-resistant tape
- Protective paper
- Heat-resistant gloves
- Nomex pad
- Heat press
- Heat-resistant gloves

RECOMMENDED SETTINGS

- Press time: 4 minutes
- Temperature: 400˚F (205˚C)
- Pressure: light to medium

SUBLIMATION SANDWICH

This diagram shows the order of the layers for pressing your project.
Refer to this visual if you need to as you follow the step-by-step instructions!

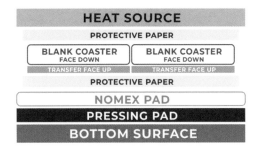

HEAT SOURCE
PROTECTIVE PAPER
BLANK COASTER FACE DOWN | BLANK COASTER FACE DOWN
TRANSFER FACE UP | TRANSFER FACE UP
PROTECTIVE PAPER
NOMEX PAD
PRESSING PAD
BOTTOM SURFACE

BEFORE YOU BEGIN

- I am using ceramic coasters for this project, which have a four-minute press time. Hardboard coasters are another popular option with a much-shorter pressing time, so make sure to consult the manufacturer's time and temperature settings before pressing.

- For this project, I added a white initial to each coaster within the design software to personalize them.

- Sublimate on the bright, shiny white side of the coaster, not the duller off-white side.

- Often, ceramic coasters are pressed face down with the printed sublimation transfer underneath the coasters instead of on top. We'll use this method in this project, but always refer to the manufacturer's recommendations.

- If you find your coasters are unevenly pressed (you have fading on one side, for example), use a green pad on top of the Nomex pad to ensure a more even press.

- Ceramic stays hot much longer than other materials. Use heat-resistant gloves if you want to remove your transfers from your coasters before they've cooled.

INSTRUCTIONS

1. Upload your images to your software and resize to fit your coasters.

2. Print your transfers, making sure to reverse your images before printing.

3. Set your heat press time and temperature.

4. Lint-roll your coasters or use alcohol and a microfiber cloth to clean them.

5. Trim your transfers to fit on your coasters.

6. Use heat-resistant tape to secure the first transfer to a coaster. Repeat for the other three coasters.

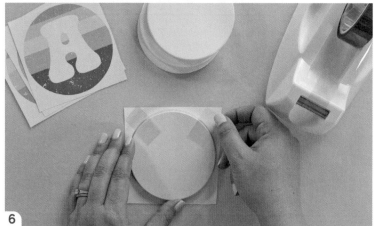

9

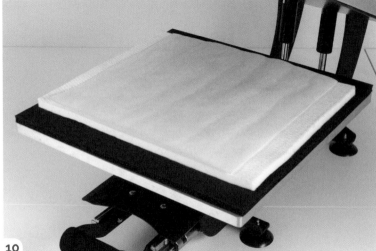

10

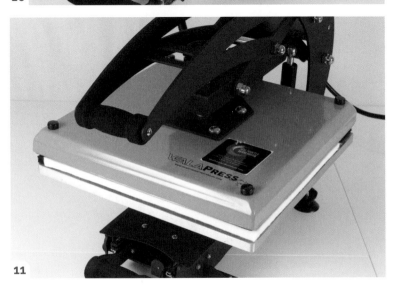

11

7. Position a Nomex pad on the bottom of your heat press (don't remove the heat press pad). Some manufacturers may not require this step.

8. Place a sheet of protective paper on top of the Nomex pad.

9. Arrange your coasters face down on the protective paper. Try to get them fairly evenly spaced so the heat press will press them evenly.

10. Place another sheet of protective paper on top of the coasters.

11. Press your coasters for the recommended time.

12. Carefully open the press and allow your coasters to cool for a bit. Remove the protective paper and transfers to reveal your coaster designs.

Metal Photo Panel

Metal photo panels bring gorgeous, vivid colors to all your images! Because the shiny metal shows through the sublimation ink, it gives your images a lustrous metallic quality that can't be achieved with a white substrate. They are particularly great for photographs, like this beachy sunset image.

TOOLS & MATERIALS

- Sublimation paper
- Sublimation photo panel
- Lint roller, or alcohol and microfiber cloth
- Heat-resistant tape
- Protective paper
- Heat press
- Heat-resistant gloves

RECOMMENDED SETTINGS

- Press time: 75 seconds
- Temperature: 400˚F (205˚C)
- Pressure: medium

SUBLIMATION SANDWICH

This diagram shows the order of the layers for pressing your project.
Refer to this visual if you need to as you follow the step-by-step instructions!

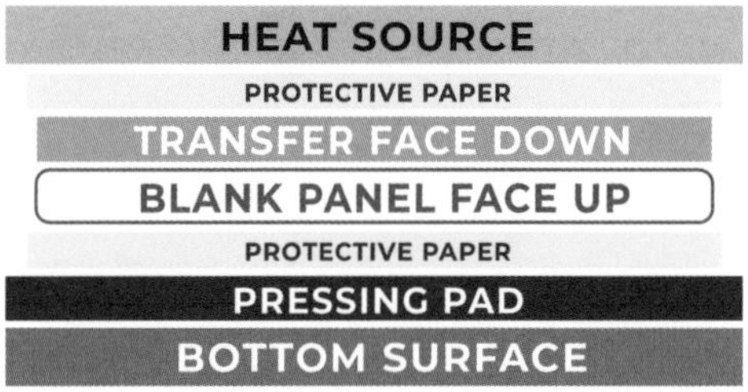

HEAT SOURCE
PROTECTIVE PAPER
TRANSFER FACE DOWN
BLANK PANEL FACE UP
PROTECTIVE PAPER
PRESSING PAD
BOTTOM SURFACE

BEFORE YOU BEGIN

- Use a weeding hook or other tool to carefully peel up the plastic coating from the photo panel before using it.

- Most metal photo panels have a watermark on the back to make it clear which side to sublimate.

INSTRUCTIONS

1. Upload your image to your software and resize to fit your photo panel.

2. Print your transfer, making sure to reverse your image before printing.

3. Set your heat press time and temperature.

4. Peel off any protective film from your photo panel.

5. Lint-roll your photo panel or use alcohol and a microfiber cloth to clean it.

6. Trim your transfer to fit your photo panel.

7. Place your photo panel face down on your printed sublimation transfer, making sure it's centered. Use heat-resistant tape to secure your transfer to the photo panel.

8. Place a sheet of protective paper on the bottom pad of your heat press.

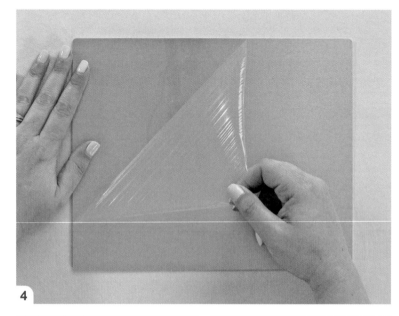

4

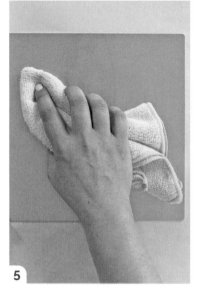

5

7

9. Set your photo panel on the protective paper with the photo panel facing up and the transfer facing down.

10. Place a sheet of protective paper on top of the photo panel.

11. Press your photo panel.

12. Carefully open the press and allow your photo to cool for a bit. Remove the protective paper and transfer to reveal your finished photo panel.

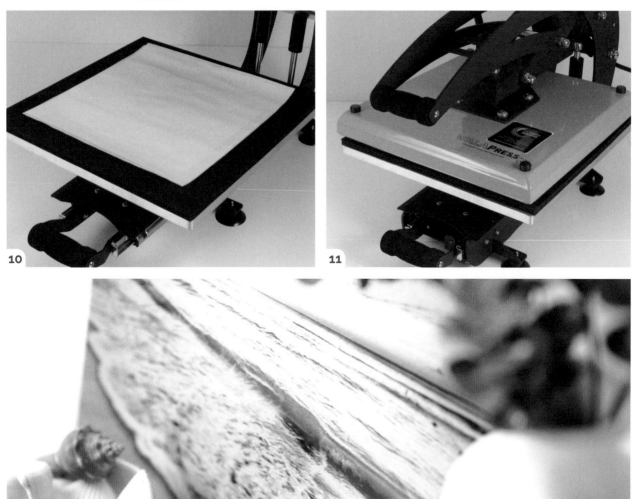

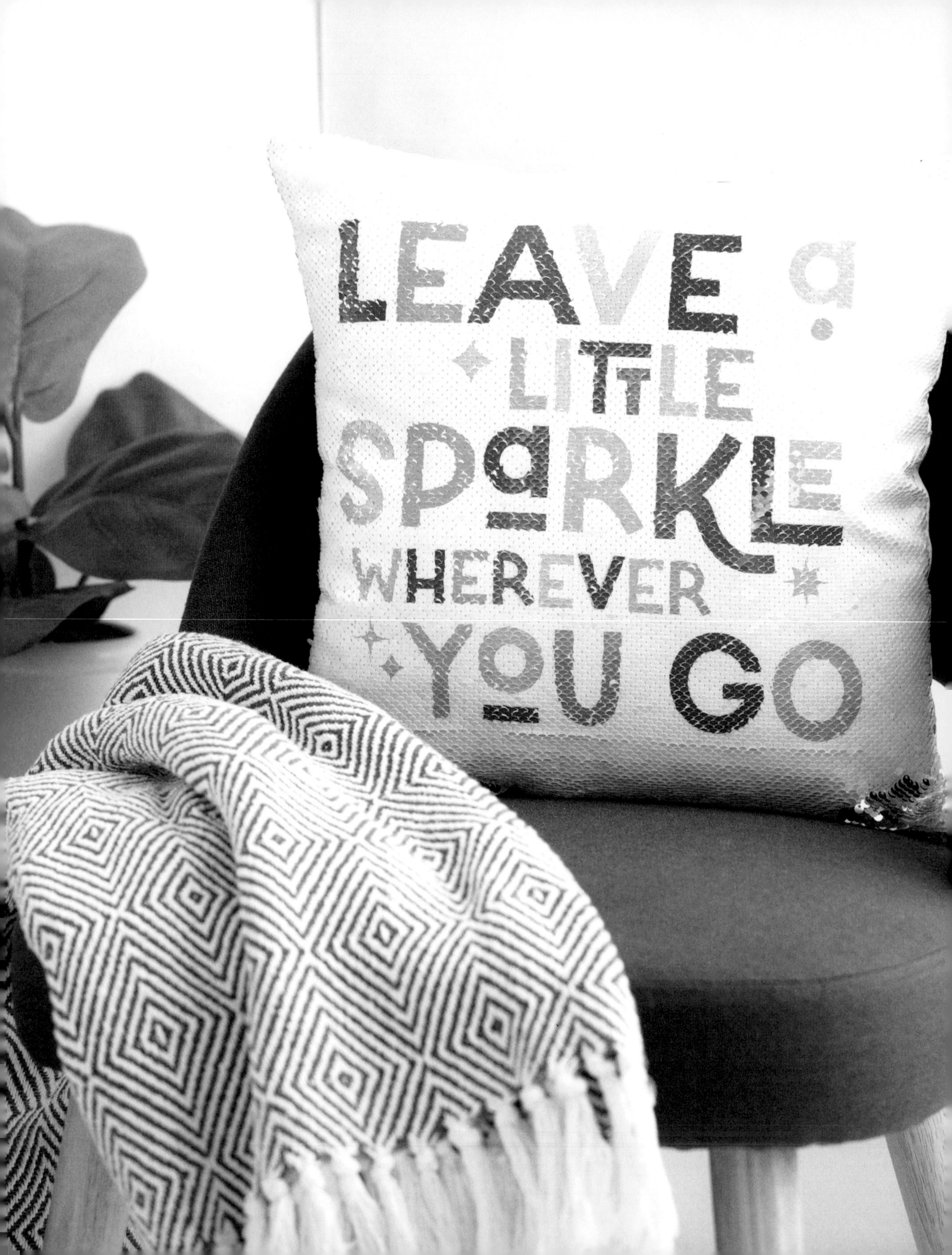
LEAVE a
LITTLE
SPaRKLE
WHEREVER
YOU GO

Sequined Pillow Cover ✦

Who doesn't love a little sparkle? A sequined pillow cover makes a great gift for kids and teens and is an easier project than you might think. Flip the sequins one way for a solid color, and then flip them over to reveal your design!

TOOLS & MATERIALS

- Sublimation paper
- Sublimation sequined pillow cover
- Lint roller
- Pressing pillow
- Heat-resistant tape
- Protective paper
- Heat press
- Heat-resistant gloves

RECOMMENDED SETTINGS

- Press time: 45 seconds
- Temperature: 385˚F (195˚C)
- Pressure: medium

SUBLIMATION SANDWICH

This diagram shows the order of the layers for pressing your project. Refer to this visual if you need to as you follow the step-by-step instructions!

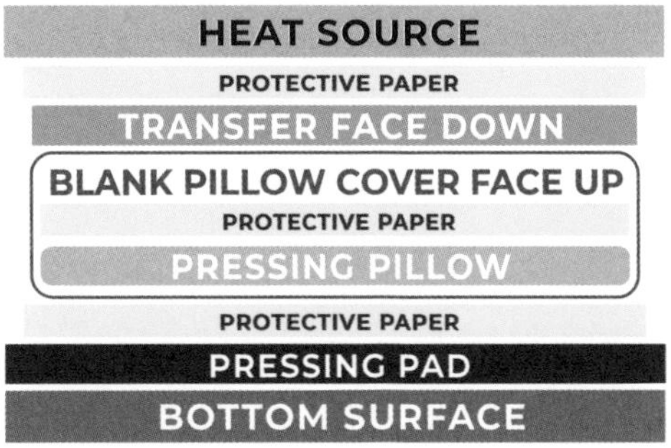

HEAT SOURCE
PROTECTIVE PAPER
TRANSFER FACE DOWN
BLANK PILLOW COVER FACE UP
PROTECTIVE PAPER
PRESSING PILLOW
PROTECTIVE PAPER
PRESSING PAD
BOTTOM SURFACE

BEFORE YOU BEGIN

- If your pillow cover has a plastic zipper, make sure it is hanging off the side of the press so it doesn't warp or melt when you press it.

- To print an extra-large image, use tabloid-sized 11" x 17" (28 x 43 cm) paper if your printer supports it.

INSTRUCTIONS

1. Upload your image to your software and resize to fit your pillow cover.

2. Print your transfer, making sure to reverse your image before printing.

3. Set your heat press time and temperature.

4. Use your hands to flip all the sequins on your pillow cover so the white side of the sequins is showing. If needed, use a weeding hook or other tool to flip over any stubborn sequins.

5. Lint-roll your pillow cover to remove any debris.

6. Slide a pressing pillow and a sheet of protective paper between the two layers of your pillow cover to raise the pressing surface and prevent bleed-through.

7. Trim your transfer to fit your pillow cover.

8. Place your transfer face down on your pillow cover. Use a ruler or measuring tape to make sure it is centered.

4

5

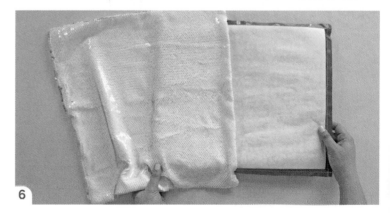

6

9

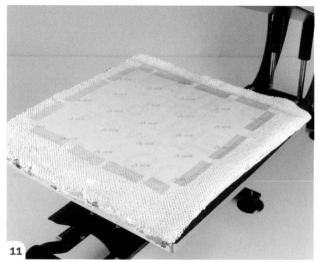

11

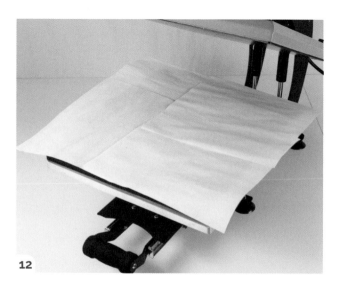

12

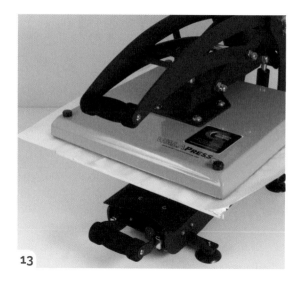

13

9. Use heat-resistant tape to secure your transfer to the pillow cover.

10. Place a sheet of protective paper on the bottom pad of your heat press.

11. Position your pillow cover (with the protective paper and pressing pillow) on the protective paper.

12. Place a sheet of protective paper on top of the pillow cover. Cover the entire pillow cover with protective paper, not just the transfer, to protect the sequins from the heat platen. Use multiple overlapping sheets of paper if necessary.

13. Press your pillow cover.

14. Carefully open the press and allow your pillow to cool for a bit, then remove the protective paper. Then very carefully remove the tape so you don't accidentally pull off any of the sequins, and reveal your final pillow cover.

15. Insert a pillow form to complete your project.

Decorative Flag

Garden flags are one of my favorite projects. You can make them for every season or holiday and swap them out as often as you'd like. Throwing a graduation party? Celebrate with a flag! Your spouse is retiring? Share the news with a flag! Selling Girl Scout cookies? Let your neighbors know with a flag! They are inexpensive to buy and are easy to store as well. Plus, they work just as well as a decorative wall hanging for indoor use!

TOOLS & MATERIALS

- Sublimation paper
- Sublimation garden flag
- Paper trimmer, or rotary cutter with acrylic ruler and self-healing cutting mat
- Lint roller
- Heat-resistant tape
- Protective paper
- Heat press
- Heat-resistant gloves

RECOMMENDED SETTINGS

- Pre-press time: 15 seconds
- Press time: 90 seconds
- Temperature: 400°F (205°C)
- Pressure: medium

SUBLIMATION SANDWICH

This diagram shows the order of the layers for pressing your project. Refer to this visual if you need to as you follow the step-by-step instructions!

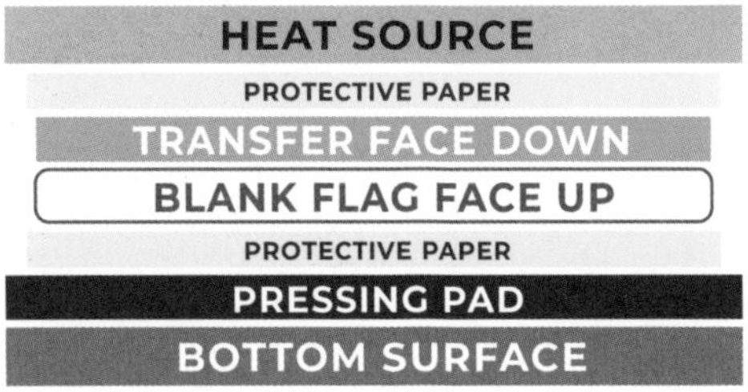

HEAT SOURCE
PROTECTIVE PAPER
TRANSFER FACE DOWN
BLANK FLAG FACE UP
PROTECTIVE PAPER
PRESSING PAD
BOTTOM SURFACE

BEFORE YOU BEGIN

- To print an extra-large image, use tabloid-sized 11" x 17" (28 x 43 cm) paper if your printer supports it.

INSTRUCTIONS

1. Upload your image to your software and resize to fit your flag.

2. Print your transfer, making sure to reverse your image before printing.

3. Set your heat press time and temperature.

4. Lint-roll your flag to remove any debris.

5. Position your flag on the bottom of your heat press plate.

6. Smooth out the flag so it's wrinkle-free and pre-press your flag for 15 seconds to remove any moisture. Let cool for a bit, then remove the flag from the press.

7. Trim your transfer to fit your flag.

8. Place your printed sublimation transfer face down on your flag. Use a ruler or measuring tape to make sure it is centered.

9. Use heat-resistant tape to secure your transfer to the flag.

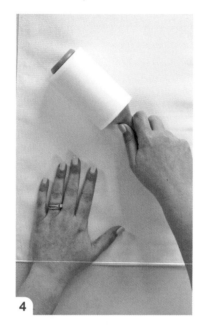

4

9

11

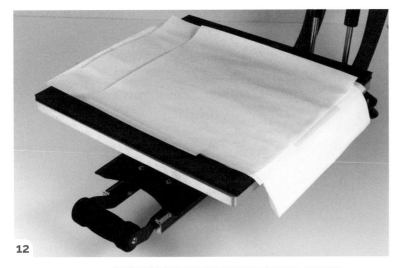

12

13

10. Place a sheet of protective paper on the bottom pad of your heat press.

11. Set your flag on the protective paper with the flag facing up and the transfer facing down.

12. Place a sheet of protective paper on top of the transfer. Use multiple overlapping sheets of paper if necessary.

13. Press your flag for the recommended time.

14. Carefully open the press and allow your flag to cool for a bit. Remove the protective paper and transfer to reveal your finished flag.

Photo Slate

Elevate your photos with these beautiful photo slates! Add an acrylic easel to make the perfect gift for grandparents and other loved ones. Photo slates can be a bit tricky to get right, but with the tips below, you'll be making them for yourself and your friends and family in no time.

TOOLS & MATERIALS

- Sublimation paper
- Sublimation photo slate
- Lint roller, or alcohol and microfiber cloth
- Heat-resistant tape
- Protective paper
- Green pad
- Heat press
- Heat-resistant gloves

RECOMMENDED SETTINGS

- Hover time: 2 minutes
- Press time: 4–5 minutes
- Temperature: 400˚F (205˚C)
- Pressure: heavy

SUBLIMATION SANDWICH

This diagram shows the order of the layers for pressing your project. Refer to this visual if you need to as you follow the step-by-step instructions!

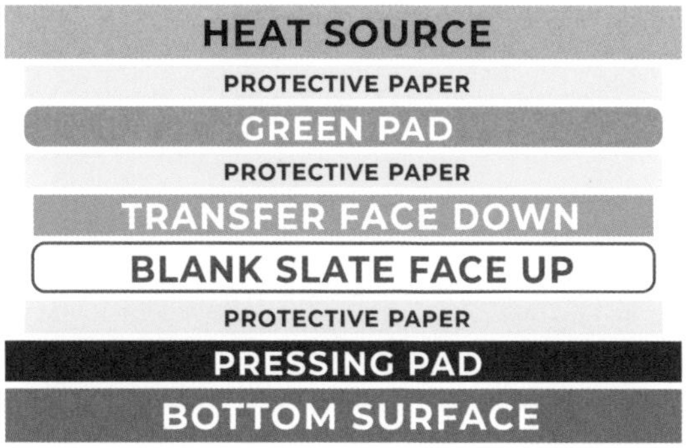

HEAT SOURCE
PROTECTIVE PAPER
GREEN PAD
PROTECTIVE PAPER
TRANSFER FACE DOWN
BLANK SLATE FACE UP
PROTECTIVE PAPER
PRESSING PAD
BOTTOM SURFACE

BEFORE YOU BEGIN

- Moisture is the enemy of photo slates. Make sure you're using your heat press to dry out your slate before you add your transfer. Moisture in your photo slate blocks the ink from bonding with the poly coating, leaving your image light and mottled. See the photo on page 79 for what this looks like.

- If you're doing multiple slates and want to save time, you can preheat them in a convection or toaster oven. Just use the "warm" setting, around 180°F (82°C). Put the slates in 30 minutes ahead of time and keep them in the oven until you're ready to press.

- The green pad allows the sublimation transfer to press into the uneven edge of the photo slate. It also protects your slate from the hard plate of the press.

- Photo slates stay hot much longer than other materials. Use heat-resistant gloves if you want to remove your transfer from your project before it's cooled.

INSTRUCTIONS

1. Upload your image to your software and resize to fit your slate.

2. Print your transfer, making sure to reverse your image before printing.

3. Set your heat press temperature.

4. Lint-roll your photo slate or use alcohol and a microfiber cloth to clean it.

5. Hover your heat press plate 1" (2.5 cm) over your slate for two minutes to help remove moisture from the slate.

6. Trim your transfer to fit your slate.

7. Use heat-resistant tape to secure your transfer to the slate.

4

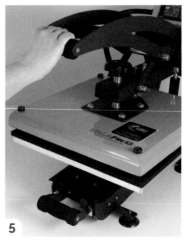
5

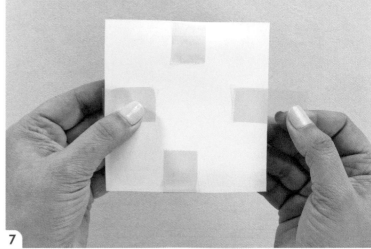
7

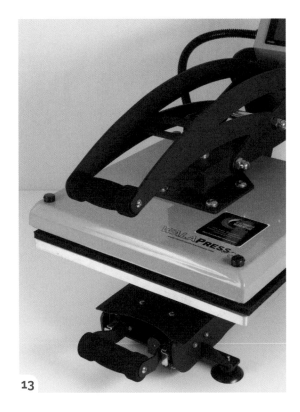

8. Place a sheet of protective paper on the bottom pad of your heat press.

9. Set your photo slate on the protective paper with the slate facing up and the transfer facing down.

10. Place a sheet of protective paper on top of the transfer.

11. Add the green pad on top of the protective paper.

12. Place a sheet of protective paper on top of the green pad.

13. Press your photo slate.

14. Carefully open the press and allow your photo slate to cool for a bit. Remove the protective paper and transfer to reveal your beautiful photo slate.

15. Add the rubber feet to the back of the photo slate so it doesn't slide around.

Stickers

An electronic cutting machine like a Cricut or Silhouette expands the number of projects you can craft with your sublimation printer. You'll print your images on regular sublimation paper and transfer them to a sublimation sticker sheet using your heat press! Then use your cutting machine's print-then-cut feature to cut around the edges of the sticker designs so you can peel them up and put them on just about anything.

TOOLS & MATERIALS

- Sublimation sticker sheets
- Sublimation paper
- Lint roller
- Heat-resistant tape
- Protective paper
- Cutting machine with print-then-cut capabilities
- Standard cutting machine mat
- Brayer
- Heat press
- Heat-resistant gloves

RECOMMENDED SETTINGS

- Press time: 30 seconds
- Temperature: 380°F (195°C)
- Pressure: medium

SUBLIMATION SANDWICH

This diagram shows the order of the layers for pressing your project. Refer to this visual if you need to as you follow the step-by-step instructions!

HEAT SOURCE
PROTECTIVE PAPER
TRANSFER FACE DOWN
BLANK STICKER SHEET FACE UP
PROTECTIVE PAPER
PRESSING PAD
BOTTOM SURFACE

BEFORE YOU BEGIN

- I am using my Cricut Explore 3 and Cricut Design Space's Print Then Cut feature, but you can create this project using similar steps with any cutting machine that has print-then-cut capabilities.

- You may not think that sticker paper can get that hot, but it's very hot right out of the press! Use heat-resistant gloves.

- If your image is backward after pressing it, the image may be reversed in your cutting machine software AND in your printer settings, which cancel each other out. Turn the mirror setting on or off in your cutting machine software to compensate for this double-mirroring issue.

- No matter what you do, the sticker paper will curl after pressing. Just be aware that it's totally normal.

- If you don't have a cutting machine, you can cut around the edges of the stickers by hand with scissors.

- These stickers are kiss cut, meaning that they peel off the backing sheet like a regular sheet of stickers. If you want to cut all the way through the material to create a sticker than is die cut rather than kiss cut, use a medium cardstock setting.

INSTRUCTIONS

1. Upload the images to Cricut Design Space. I have designed these files with a white offset around the edge of the image, but you can add an offset using the Offset tool if you're using different images.

2. Resize your images based on how large you want your final stickers to be.

3. Click "Make It" in the upper right. Then arrange your images on your mat to make the most of the Print Then Cut area.

4. While still in the Prepare screen, click the mirror slider to reverse your images, and click "Continue."

5. In the Make screen, you'll be prompted to print your image. Print your image on regular sublimation paper.

6. Set your heat press time and temperature.

7. Place your printed sublimation transfer face down on the sticker sheet.

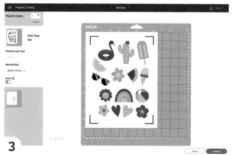

8

8. Use heat-resistant tape to secure your transfer to the sticker sheet.

9. Place a sheet of protective paper on the bottom pad of your heat press.

10. Set your sticker sheet on the protective paper with the sticker sheet facing up and the transfer facing down.

11. Place a sheet of protective paper on top of the transfer.

12. Press your sticker paper.

13. Carefully open the press and remove the protective paper and transfer from the sticker sheet. Your sticker sheet will curl—this is normal.

14. Place the sticker sheet face up on a standard cutting machine mat, using the brayer to help it stick.

15. Load the mat into your Cricut (or other cutting machine) and select "light cardstock" as the material setting in Cricut Design Space.

16. Press the blinking button on your machine to prompt it to cut around the edges of your stickers.

17. Remove the sticker sheet from the cutting mat and peel up your stickers to use them.

10

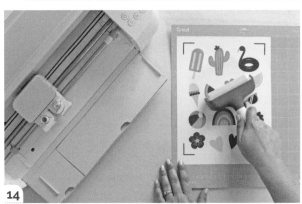

14

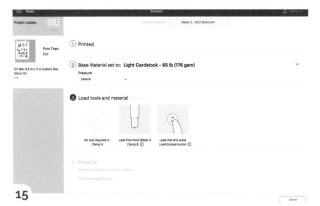

15

16

Tapered Tumbler ♥

While straight-sided tumblers are fairly straightforward, making a tapered tumbler can be a bit complicated. The key is finding the right template for your project so when it's cut, it fits around your tumbler perfectly. Even then, you can often end up with blurring and other image issues because of variations in the taper. One way around this is to use a smaller single image on each side, or a bunch of smaller images to create a pattern, like I did with these hearts. Tapered tumblers and other oddly shaped blanks are usually made using the convection oven method featured here.

TOOLS & MATERIALS

- Sublimation paper
- Tapered sublimation tumbler
- Scissors
- Lint roller, or alcohol and microfiber cloth
- Heat-resistant tape
- Shrink-wrap sleeve
- Convection oven
- Nomex pad (optional)
- Heat-resistant gloves

RECOMMENDED SETTINGS

- Time in oven: 6 minutes; rotate halfway through
- Temperature: 375˚F (190˚C)
- Pressure: N/A

SUBLIMATION SANDWICH

This diagram shows the order of the layers for pressing your project.
Refer to this visual if you need to as you follow the step-by-step instructions!

CONVECTION OVEN

BLANK TUMBLER

TRANSFER FACE IN

SHRINK-WRAP SLEEVE

NOMEX PAD (OPTIONAL)

BEFORE YOU BEGIN

- For this project, I'm using a tapered tumbler, but you can buy a wide variety of sublimation blanks and different sizes of shrink-wrap sleeve to expand the types of sublimation projects you can make in your convection oven.

- Remove the lid and the straw before sublimating the tumbler.

- Other tutorials have you use a heat gun to preshrink your shrink-wrap sleeve, but I haven't found this necessary. The moment it's in the oven, the sleeve shrinks up in the heat.

- For many tapered tumblers, you'll need larger 8 ½" x 14" (22 x 35 cm) paper, which you can usually print using the bypass tray in your printer.

- If you find the rack in your convection oven is leaving marks on your tumblers, place a Nomex pad on the rack to prevent this issue.

- Don't wait for your tumbler to cool before removing the shrink-wrap. It's much easier to remove it while it's still hot.

- Do not wash your sublimated tumbler in the dishwasher. The dishwasher can ruin the vacuum sealing on the tumbler.

INSTRUCTIONS

1. Upload your image to your software and resize to fit your project. I'm using a bunch of hearts, but you can use any smaller images with this method.

2. Print your transfers, making sure to reverse your images before printing.

3. Preheat your convection oven. Add a Nomex pad to the rack if you'd like.

4. Lint-roll your tumbler or use alcohol and a microfiber cloth to clean it.

5. Trim around the edges of your images using scissors.

6. Tape your images to your tumbler in a random pattern.

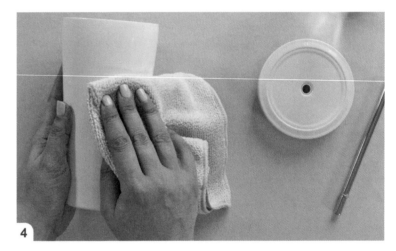

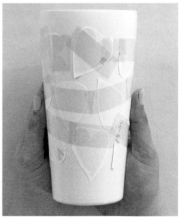

7. Slide your tumbler inside the shrink-wrap sleeve. Center it inside the sleeve.

8. Place your tumbler inside your convection oven on its side. Set the timer.

9. Rotate your tumbler 180 degrees halfway through the oven time.

10. Wearing your heat-resistant gloves, remove the tumbler from the oven. Then remove the shrink-wrap while it is still hot. Scissors or a weeding hook can be helpful.

11. Wait a few minutes for the tumbler to cool, then remove the transfer to reveal your image.

12. Add your lid and straw and you have a finished tumbler.

Glass Cutting Board

Looking for another impressive gift? A glass cutting board is perfect for your favorite chef! Add an inspirational quote, your family's name and monogram, or a handwritten recipe that's been handed down generation to generation. And yes, they are food safe!

TOOLS & MATERIALS

- Sublimation paper
- Sublimation glass cutting board
- Lint roller, or alcohol and microfiber cloth
- Heat-resistant spray or tape
- Protective paper
- Heat press
- Heat-resistant gloves
- Heat-resistant mat

RECOMMENDED SETTINGS

- Press time: 4 minutes
- Temperature: 400˚F (205˚C)
- Pressure: heavy

SUBLIMATION SANDWICH

This diagram shows the order of the layers for pressing your project. Refer to this visual if you need to as you follow the step-by-step instructions!

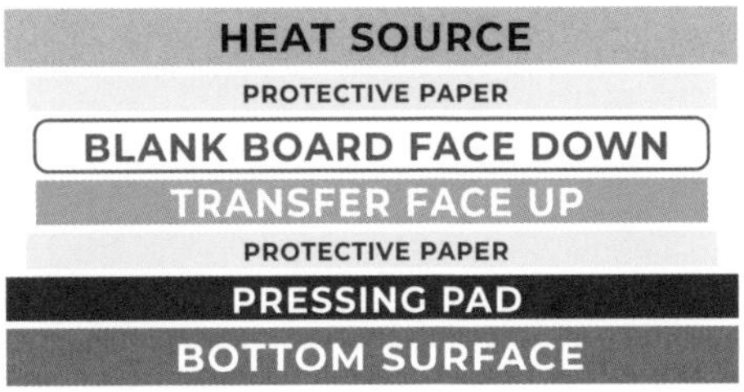

HEAT SOURCE
PROTECTIVE PAPER
BLANK BOARD FACE DOWN
TRANSFER FACE UP
PROTECTIVE PAPER
PRESSING PAD
BOTTOM SURFACE

BEFORE YOU BEGIN

- This is one of the few instances where you do NOT want to mirror your image when printing. Because this is being pressed from the back, it will look correct when viewed through the glass.

- For this project, I'm showing how to use heat-resistant adhesive spray, but you can use tape if you'd prefer.

- Often, glass cutting boards are pressed face down with the printed sublimation transfer underneath the cutting board

- instead of on top. We'll use this method in this project, but always refer to the manufacturer's recommendations.

- Glass stays hot much longer than other materials. Use heat-resistant gloves if you want to remove your transfer from your cutting board before it's cooled.

- Do not wash your sublimated glass cutting board on sanitize mode in the dishwasher. The high temperatures can re-sublimate and fade the ink.

INSTRUCTIONS

1. Upload your image to your software and resize to fit your cutting board.

2. Print your transfer. Do NOT mirror your image.

3. Set your heat press time and temperature.

4. Lint-roll your cutting board or use alcohol and a microfiber cloth to clean it.

5. Trim your transfer to fit your cutting board.

6. Lightly spray your transfer with the heat-resistant adhesive spray.

7. Center the transfer and stick it to the white side of the cutting board.

8. Place a sheet of protective paper on the bottom pad of your heat press.

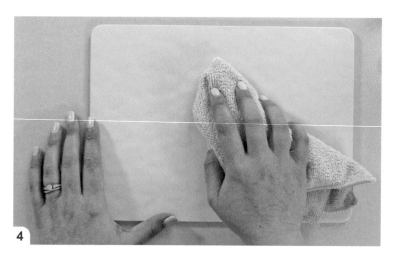

4

6

7

9

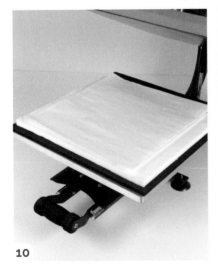

10

11

9. Position your cutting board on the protective paper with the cutting board facing down and the transfer facing up.

10. Place a sheet of protective paper on top of the cutting board.

11. Press your cutting board for the recommended time.

12. Carefully open the press and allow your cutting board to cool for a bit. Remove the protective paper and transfer to reveal your gorgeous final result.

13. Add the rubber feet to the back of the cutting board so it doesn't slide around.

"Scrap" Earrings

Want to make use of sublimation prints you accidentally printed at the wrong size or orientation? These "off" prints are perfect for sublimating smaller projects like earrings, key chains, ornaments, and more! You can also resize patterns and backgrounds to make all sorts of fun projects.

TOOLS & MATERIALS

- Sublimation paper
- Sublimation earrings and earring findings
- Lint roller, or alcohol and microfiber cloth
- Scissors
- Heat-resistant tape
- Protective paper
- Handheld heat press
- Heat-resistant mat
- Heat-resistant gloves
- Jewelry pliers

RECOMMENDED SETTINGS

- Press time: 60 seconds
- Temperature: 400°F (205°C)
- Pressure: medium

SUBLIMATION SANDWICH

This diagram shows the order of the layers for pressing your project. Refer to this visual if you need to as you follow the step-by-step instructions!

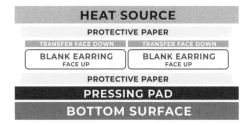

HEAT SOURCE
PROTECTIVE PAPER
TRANSFER FACE DOWN | TRANSFER FACE DOWN
BLANK EARRING FACE UP | BLANK EARRING FACE UP
PROTECTIVE PAPER
PRESSING PAD
BOTTOM SURFACE

BEFORE YOU BEGIN

• While you can make earrings with a larger heat press, a handheld press like this small EasyPress makes making them even easier.

INSTRUCTIONS

1. Use an "off-print" transfer or upload your image to your software and resize to fit your earrings.

2. If printing, print your transfer, making sure to reverse your image before printing.

3. Set your heat press time and temperature.

4. Lint-roll your earrings or use alcohol and a microfiber cloth to clean them.

5. You can either trim your transfer to fit around your earrings or simply place your earrings face down on your transfer.

6. Use heat-resistant tape to secure your transfer to your earrings.

7. Position a sheet of protective paper on your heat-resistant mat.

8. Set your earrings on the protective paper with the earrings facing up and the transfer facing down.

9. Place a sheet of protective paper on top of the transfer.

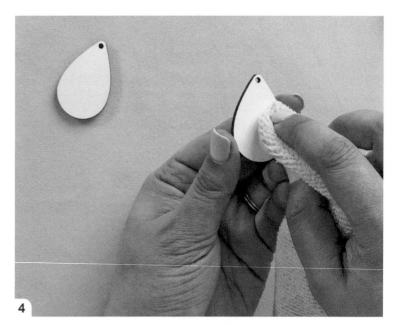

4

6

9

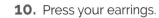

10. Press your earrings.

11. Remove the press and allow your earrings to cool for a bit. Remove the protective paper and transfers to reveal your designs.

12. Use pliers to add the findings your earrings.

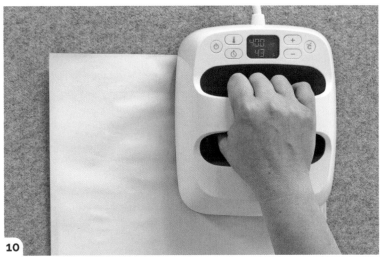

10

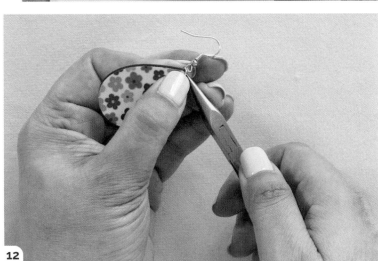

12

Wood Sign

Many crafters love the look of wood home décor items and other blanks, but wood doesn't have the poly content needed for sublimation. One of my favorite tricks for sublimating on many non-poly materials is lamination sheets. These projects are a bit shiny, but overall they create a more rustic look than regular sublimation blanks.

TOOLS & MATERIALS

- Sublimation paper
- 8" (20 cm) wood round
- Sanding block
- Lint roller
- Lamination pouch
- Heat-resistant tape
- Protective paper
- Craft knife
- Self-healing cutting mat
- Nomex pad
- Heat press
- Heat-resistant gloves

RECOMMENDED SETTINGS

- Lamination press time: 15 seconds
- Lamination temperature: 320°F (160°C)
- Sublimation press time: 50 seconds
- Sublimation temperature: 375°F (190°C)
- Pressure: medium

LAMINATION SANDWICH

HEAT SOURCE
PROTECTIVE PAPER
LAMINATE SHEET DULL SIDE DOWN / SHINY SIDE UP
WOOD ROUND FACE UP
PROTECTIVE PAPER
NOMEX PAD
PRESSING PAD
BOTTOM SURFACE

SUBLIMATION SANDWICH

HEAT SOURCE
PROTECTIVE PAPER
TRANSFER FACE DOWN
WOOD ROUND FACE UP
PROTECTIVE PAPER
PRESSING PAD
BOTTOM SURFACE

These diagrams show the order of the layers for pressing your project. Refer to this visual if you need to as you follow the step-by-step instructions!

BEFORE YOU BEGIN

- The smoother your wood round, the better your image will look. Don't use a highly textured wood—the lamination sheet and image won't transfer well.

- You can also paint your wood white before pressing the lamination sheet. Make sure your paint dries for at least 48 hours, and then press your wood for 1 minute at 350°F (175°C) to release any remaining moisture from the paint.

- The laminate pouch will have two layers. Cut open the pouch on one side and lay the pouch flat. The dull side has the adhesive and should be the side you place face down on your wood round.

- After pressing, place something heavy, such as a stack of books, on top of your wood round to prevent it from warping.

INSTRUCTIONS

1. Lightly sand your wood round to create a smooth surface for sublimating.

2. Upload your image to your software and resize to fit your wood round.

3. Print your transfer, making sure to reverse your image before printing.

4. Set your heat press time and temperature for the lamination sheet.

5. Lint-roll your wood round to remove any debris.

6. Open the laminate pouch and use a craft knife to cut a piece of the correct side of the laminate sheet just larger than your wood round.

7. Place a Nomex pad on the bottom pad of your heat press.

8. Place a sheet of protective paper on top of the Nomex pad.

9. Place the wood round in your heat press with the laminate sheet on top. Make sure that the laminate around the edge of the wood round has protective paper under it so it doesn't adhere to the pad.

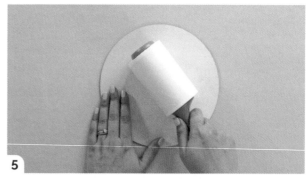

5

6

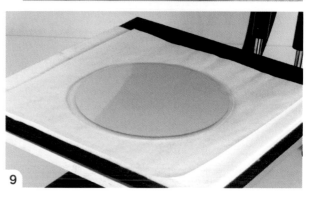

9

10

11

13

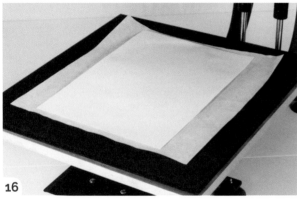

16

17

10. Press your laminate sheet.

11. Wait for the wood round to cool, then flip the wood round over and use a craft knife on a self-healing cutting mat to remove the excess laminate from around the edge of the wood round.

12. Place your wood round face down on your printed sublimation transfer, making sure it's centered.

13. Use heat-resistant tape to secure your transfer to the wood round.

14. Reset your heat press to the sublimation time and temperature.

15. Place a new sheet of protective paper on the bottom pad of the heat press.

16. Set your wood round on the protective paper with the wood round facing up and the transfer facing down.

17. Place a sheet of protective paper on top of the wood round.

18. Press your wood round.

19. Carefully open the press and allow your wood round to cool for a bit. Remove the protective paper and transfer to reveal your final sign.

20. Use the sanding block to sand down any remaining rough edges.

Snow Globe Tumbler

Take your beverages up a notch with this trendy sublimated snow globe tumbler! Sublimate an image on the glass and then fill with a sparkly glitter solution. These are perfect for gifts and are sure to be a hit with the customers of your crafty small business.

TOOLS & MATERIALS

- Sublimation paper
- Sublimation snow globe tumbler
- Paper trimmer, or rotary cutter with acrylic ruler and self-healing cutting mat
- Lint roller, or alcohol and microfiber cloth
- Heat-resistant tape
- Protective paper
- Heat-resistant gloves
- Tumbler press
- Chunky glitter
- Fine glitter
- 2 oz. (60 mL) vegetable glycerin (plus extra if needed)
- 2 oz. (60 mL) water (plus extra if needed)
- Cup
- Popsicle stick or other stirrer
- Plastic syringe
- Small paintbrush
- Alcohol and cotton pad
- UV resin kit with UV light

RECOMMENDED SETTINGS

- Press time: 150 seconds
- Temperature: 360°F (180°C)
- Pressure: light to medium

SUBLIMATION SANDWICH

This diagram shows the order of the layers for pressing your project.
Refer to this visual if you need to as you follow the step-by-step instructions!

BLANK TUMBLER

TRANSFER FACE IN

PROTECTIVE PAPER

HEAT SOURCE

BEFORE YOU BEGIN

- These tumblers have a premade hole in the bottom specifically for adding a glitter solution.

- You can also use the shrink-wrap method in a convection oven for this project, like I used with the tapered tumbler.

- Remove the lid and the straw before sublimating the tumbler.

- Using a rotary cutter with an acrylic ruler and self-healing cutting mat is the best way to trim your transfer because you can cut off the narrowest strips of your transfer. You want the transfer to wrap around your tumbler so the edges overlap ever so

slightly. That way you don't have a seam down the side of the tumbler. If you trim it too small, reprint and retrim your transfer.

- You want a 1:1 ratio of water and vegetable glycerin. I suggest starting with 2 oz. (60 mL) of each, but you may need more, depending on your tumbler. If needed, mix more solution.

- How much glitter to use is up to you. I used about 2 teaspoons each of three different glitters.

- Do not wash your sublimated tumbler in the dishwasher. The washing can unseal the resin.

INSTRUCTIONS

1. Upload your image to your software and resize to fit your tumbler.

2. Print your transfer, making sure to reverse your image before printing.

3. Set your tumbler press time and temperature.

4. Lint-roll your tumbler or use alcohol and a microfiber cloth to clean it.

5. Trim your printed sublimation transfer to fit your tumbler.

6. Wrap your transfer around your tumbler as tightly as possible and secure the seam with strips of heat-resistant tape. Tape the top and bottom of the tumbler as well, using your thumbs to really press the transfer onto the curved edges of the tumbler.

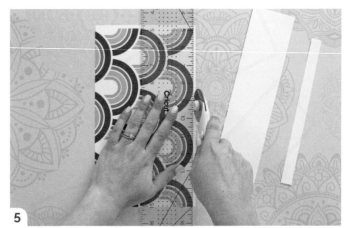

5

7

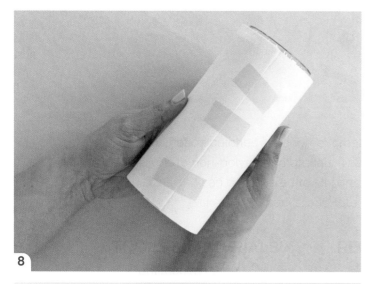

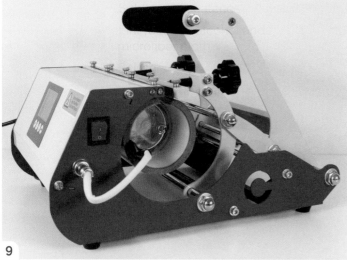

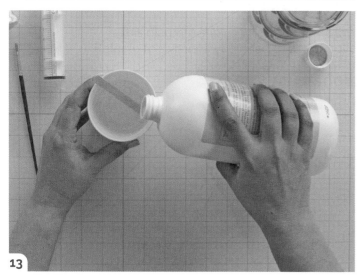

7. Add a long piece of tape along the seam of your transfer. Run your thumbnail along the seam to press the tape into the seam and minimize blowout.

8. Wrap two sheets of protective paper tightly around your tumbler and secure with heat-resistant tape.

9. Press your tumbler for the recommended time, rotating the tumbler 180 degrees halfway through the pressing time.

10. Wearing your heat-resistant gloves, carefully open the tumbler press, remove the tumbler, and set it on a heat-resistant surface.

11. Wait a few minutes for the tumbler to cool, then remove the transfer to reveal your image.

12. Flip the tumbler over so the bottom is facing up and the hole in the glass is accessible.

13. Mix together about 2 oz. (60 mL) of vegetable glycerin and 2 oz. (60 mL) of water in a small cup. Stir until combined. Do not shake. Try to limit the air bubbles you create.

14. Use the syringe to draw up about one-third (20 mL) of your solution. Carefully press the syringe's plunger to release the solution through the hole and into the tumbler. You may find tilting the tumbler slightly helps.

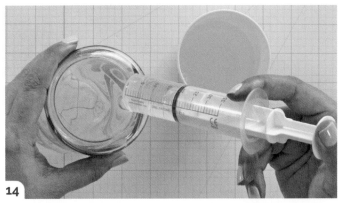

15. To add glitter, pour a bit of glitter on the base of the tumbler and use a small paintbrush to sweep the glitter into the hole. Repeat with each glitter color.

16. Use the syringe to fill the tumbler the rest of the way with the solution. Fill the tumbler as full as possible to avoid air bubbles.

17. For the last bit of the tumbler, use only water and tilt your tumbler so the remaining air bubble is under the hole. Water has a lower viscosity and can fill up that last little bit of the tumbler more easily than the 50/50 solution. It mixes in the first time you shake your tumbler.

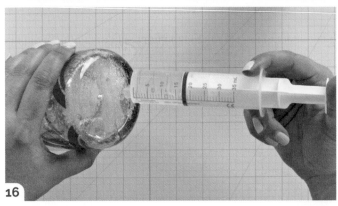

18. Clean the bottom of your tumbler with an alcohol-soaked cotton ball.

19

20

19. Remove the cap of the UV resin and squeeze a small amount over the hole in the bottom of the tumbler. Use a popsicle stick if needed to flatten it out. You want to make sure the hole is fully covered.

20. Use the UV light to cure your resin for 2 minutes.

21. Test the tumbler to make sure it's not leaking. Carefully tilt the tumbler. If you see solution bubbling through the resin, add another thin coat and cure again.

22. Add your lid and your straw, and you have a finished tumbler.

Zippered Pouch with Glitter HTV

Want to move beyond sublimating white polyester fabrics? You can sublimate on glitter HTV (heat-transfer vinyl)! Use this trick for adding sublimated images to cotton and dark fabrics, like this zippered pouch. For this project, I'm using a Cricut cutting machine to cut out the glitter HTV and printed sublimation transfer, but you can cut by hand for simpler designs.

TOOLS & MATERIALS

- Sublimation paper
- White glitter HTV
- Cutting machine with print-then-cut capabilities
- Standard cutting machine mat
- Weeding tool
- Zippered pouch
- Pressing pillow
- Lint roller
- Protective paper
- Heat-resistant tape
- Heat press
- Heat-resistant gloves

RECOMMENDED SETTINGS

- Pre-press time: 15 seconds
- HTV press time: 20 seconds
- HTV temperature: 320°F (160°C)
- Sublimation press time: 60 seconds
- Sublimation temperature: 375°F (190°C)
- Pressure: medium

HTV SANDWICH

| HEAT SOURCE |
| PROTECTIVE PAPER |
| **GLITTER HTV** HTV FACE DOWN / CARRIER SHEET FACE UP |
| BLANK POUCH FACE UP |
| PROTECTIVE PAPER |
| PRESSING PILLOW |
| PROTECTIVE PAPER |
| PRESSING PAD |
| BOTTOM SURFACE |

SUBLIMATION SANDWICH

| HEAT SOURCE |
| PROTECTIVE PAPER |
| TRANSFER FACE DOWN |
| BLANK POUCH FACE UP |
| PROTECTIVE PAPER |
| PRESSING PILLOW |
| PROTECTIVE PAPER |
| PRESSING PAD |
| BOTTOM SURFACE |

These diagrams show the order of the layers for pressing your project.
Refer to this visual if you need to as you follow the step-by-step instructions!

BEFORE YOU BEGIN

- I am using my Cricut Explore 3 and Cricut Design Space's Print Then Cut feature, but you can create this project using similar steps with any cutting machine that has print-then-cut capabilities.

- If you don't have a pressing pillow small enough for your project, you can also hang the zipper off the edge of the heat press so it doesn't get pressed.

- This project will wash and wear like HTV, not like sublimation. That means that it may peel, crack, or fade over time. This is the downside to using a "hack" to sublimate on non-polyester fabrics.

INSTRUCTIONS

1. Upload the "Happy" PNG file to Cricut Design Space. For the image type, click "Complex" and click "Continue."

2. Remove your background if needed and click "Apply & Continue."

3. Click "Print Then Cut Image" and click "Upload."

4. Bring the image onto your canvas and resize to fit your pouch.

5. Duplicate the image and change the second image into a cut image using the Operation dropdown menu. Your second image will change into an outlined version of your print-then-cut image.

6. Click "Make It" in the upper right corner. In the Prepare screen that follows, you'll see your two mats: one with the HTV cut image and one with the print image. Click the mirror slider for both mats.

7. Click on the HTV cut image mat and click "Continue."

8. Place your glitter HTV with the shiny side down on your cutting mat.

9. In the Make screen, connect your Cricut and choose glitter iron-on as your material setting.

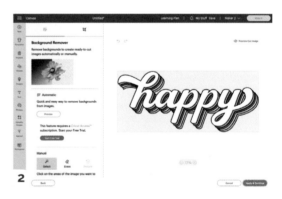

4

5

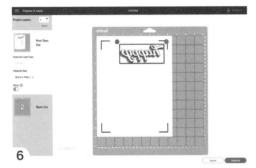

6

8

9

10. Load the cutting mat into your Cricut and press the blinking button on your machine. It will cut your HTV piece.

11. Use the weeding hook to remove the excess HTV from around your cutout.

12. Set your heat press time and temperature for the glitter HTV.

13. Lint-roll your pouch to remove debris.

14. Position your pouch on the bottom of your heat press plate.

15. Smooth out the pouch so it's wrinkle-free and pre-press it for 15 seconds to remove any moisture. Let cool for a bit, then remove the pouch from the press.

16. Place the glitter HTV on your pouch with the carrier sheet side up and the HTV side down, using a ruler or measuring tape to make sure it's centered. You can use heat-resistant tape if the carrier sheet from the HTV is not sticky enough.

17. Place a sheet of protective paper on the bottom pad of your heat press.

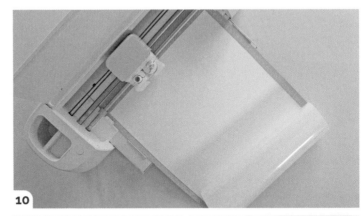

10

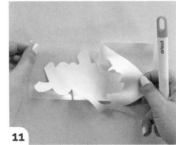

11

16

18. Press your pouch for the recommended HTV time.

19. Wait until it is completely cooled before peeling back the carrier sheet slowly and carefully. This will help minimize white outlines around your final image.

20. Reset your heat press to the sublimation time and temperature.

21. Go back to Cricut Design Space to print your sublimation image.

22. Place your printed image in the top left of your Cricut cutting mat.

23. Insert the mat into your machine. Your Cricut will scan the registration box and cut around your image.

24. Carefully peel the cut image off the mat.

19

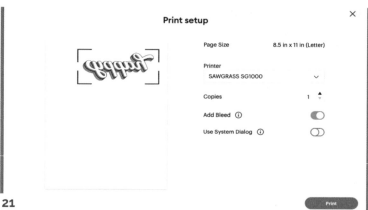
21

22

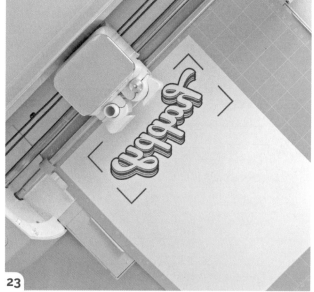
23

25.

26. Place your printed sublimation transfer face down on top of the glitter and secure with heat-resistant tape.

26. Place a piece of protective paper on the bottom pad of your heat press.

27. Position your pouch on the protective paper.

28. Place a sheet of protective paper on top of the transfer.

29. Press your pouch for the recommended sublimation time.

30. Carefully open the press and allow your pouch to cool for a bit. Remove the protective paper and transfer to reveal your final pouch project.

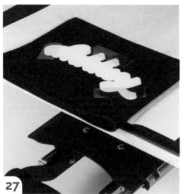

Patches

Sublimation patches are another creative way to add sublimation designs to non-polyester materials. They come in a range of shapes and sizes and can be adhered to all sorts of blanks, including hats, jean jackets, backpacks, and tote bags like this one.

TOOLS & MATERIALS

- Sublimation paper
- Sublimation patches
- Lint roller, or alcohol and microfiber cloth
- Scissors
- Heat-resistant tape
- Protective paper
- Heat press
- Heat-resistant gloves

RECOMMENDED SETTINGS

- Press time: 45 seconds
- Temperature: 385°F (195°C)
- Pressure: medium

SUBLIMATION SANDWICH

This diagram shows the order of the layers for pressing your project. Refer to this visual if you need to as you follow the step-by-step instructions!

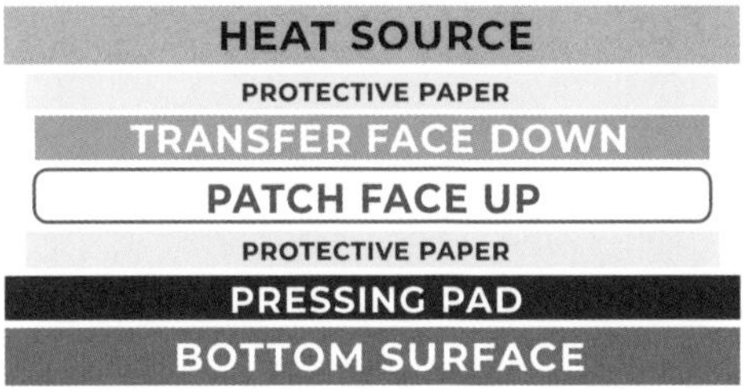

HEAT SOURCE
PROTECTIVE PAPER
TRANSFER FACE DOWN
PATCH FACE UP
PROTECTIVE PAPER
PRESSING PAD
BOTTOM SURFACE

BEFORE YOU BEGIN

INSTRUCTIONS

1. Upload your image to your software and resize to fit your patches.

2. Print your transfers, making sure to reverse your images before printing.

3. Set your heat press time and temperature.

4. Lint-roll your tote bag to remove any debris.

5. Use a pressing pillow between the layers of your tote bag to raise up your pressing surface.

6. Cut out the patch transfers carefully around the edges, getting as close to the edges of the printed image as possible.

7. Lay out your patches on your bag in an arrangement you like.

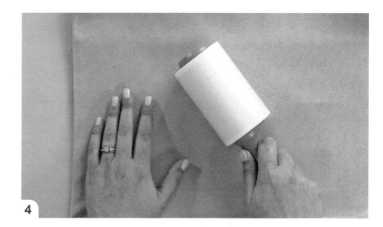

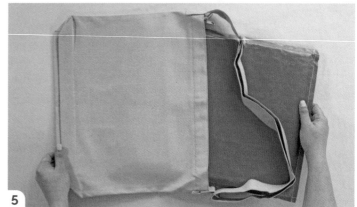

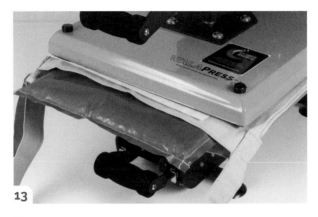

8. Peel off the paper backing from the patches to reveal the heat-activated adhesive backing.

9. Tape your transfers to your patches using heat-resistant tape. Make the pieces of tape long enough that you're also taping the patches to the tote bag.

10. Place a piece of protective paper on the bottom pad of your heat press.

11. Position your tote on the protective paper.

12. Place a sheet of protective paper on top of the transfers.

13. Press your tote bag for the recommended sublimation time.

14. Carefully open the press and allow your patches to cool for a bit. Remove the protective paper and transfers to reveal the patches on your tote bag.

How to Go Pro

If you enjoyed this book and you're having fun with sublimation, you might be considering going pro! Here are some tips to help you get started in establishing your own sublimation small business. I've broken these tips down into categories, but they aren't meant to be done in any particular order—in fact, a lot of these steps will need to be done more or less simultaneously. It's all part of the adventure!

As a small-business owner, it's up to you to do your due diligence; regulations and laws differ from state to state, and none of the tips here should be considered legal advice.

CONCEPTUALIZE YOUR BRAND

• Brainstorm a company name and do research to make sure it's not already taken by someone else. Register your business and obtain any necessary licenses or permits.

• Claim your website domain and social media handles for your business.

• Get a logo! If your design skills don't quite do the trick, look for affordable logo designers on Etsy, Creative Market, or other websites.

• Once you have your logo, develop a consistent visual brand identity, including fonts, a color scheme, and a design style.

ESTABLISH YOUR NICHE

• Think about your target audience. Identify that audience's preferences, interests, and demographics.

• With your target audience in mind, identify a specific niche for your sublimation products. Instead of trying to sell one of everything, focus on a theme or type of blank that you can consistently craft well.

• Choose how you will sell your products. Local craft fairs? Etsy or another online marketplace?

• If you're going the craft fair route, make enough products for a full booth. Create signage and set up point-of-sale payment options.

• If you're going the online route, set up an Etsy shop or other online marketplace storefront to sell your products. Optimize your shop with an appealing shop description using keywords for your products.

PRICE IT OUT

• Obtain a reseller's permit so you can buy blanks and other supplies at wholesale pricing. This will increase your profit margins.

• Start a business bank account to keep your business's finances separate from your personal finances. Talk to a CPA for more information for other financial considerations you may want to be aware of.

• Calculate your costs, including materials, equipment, labor, and shipping. Set a competitive yet profitable price for each of your products.

• If you're shipping your products, invest in packaging that reflects your brand's aesthetic and protects your products.

MAKE IT

• Perfect your products! Make sure you can consistently craft beautiful sublimation projects without errors. A big order is not the time to learn how to do a specific method.

• Set up a workspace that's organized for efficiency, and make sure it's well ventilated.

• Make the projects for your shop.

PROMOTE YOUR WORK

• Take high-quality, well-lit photographs of your products.

• Write detailed, engaging product descriptions that highlight the features and benefits of your products. Include keywords to help your customers find your products.

• Establish a social media presence to promote your business. Don't just show your products—share moments behind the scenes, helpful tips for using your products, funny craft fails, tutorials, and your small business wins.

• Start an email list. Set a consistent email schedule and offer coupons, giveaways, bonus content, or other benefits to your customers.

• Once you launch your shop, be consistent in promoting it. The algorithms reward consistency!

THINK LONG-TERM

• Ask for customer reviews. One of the biggest ways someone can be convinced to buy your product is if they know other people have already had great experiences with your products. Use any constructive criticism to improve your products.

• Regularly review your sales data, customer feedback, and marketing strategies. Then adjust your business accordingly.

• Enjoy yourself! No one wants to be miserable running their small business. If you're not enjoying yourself, take a step back and think about why. Are you crafting things you no longer enjoy crafting? Is customer service harder than you expected? Are you not making sales? Taking a bird's-eye look at what's going on in your business can help you address the pain points and make your business much more enjoyable to run.

Sublimation Glossary

Banding

Noticeable printing lines on your transfer, usually caused by low print quality, bidirectional printing, or clogged print heads.

Blank

A blank is anything you can put a sublimation design on. A few popular blanks include T-shirts, tote bags, tumblers, mugs, and pillows. See also: Substrate.

Bleed

A bleed is an extra bit of your printed image that extends beyond the trim edge of the image itself.

Blowout

A defect during pressing where the ink spreads beyond where it should be, usually caused by uneven pressure, overheating, or too much ink on the page.

Clear HTV

A heat-transfer product that allows you to sublimate on non-poly blanks.

CMYK

Cyan, magenta, yellow, black: these are the four ink colors most commonly used in sublimation printing.

Convection Oven

A small oven that can be used to heat mugs and other blanks with sublimation transfers. Do not use the same convection oven for sublimation and food.

Corel

A paid software program used for sublimation design and printing.

Decal

The printed page out of a sublimation printer. See also: Sublimation Transfer.

Deckled Edge

Ripping around a sublimation transfer versus cutting with scissors. This can help prevent press lines in your finished project.

Dwell Time

The amount of time your blank is touching the heat press platen. Also called the press time.

Dye

A substance used to color a substrate. In the case of sublimation, this is usually simply called ink, but you may see sublimation referred to as "dye sublimation."

EasyPress

A handheld heat press made by Cricut. The EasyPress 2 and EasyPress 3 can be used for sublimation. The original EasyPress does not get hot enough.

EasyPress Mat

The EasyPress mat is used in conjunction with the EasyPress as a safe pressing surface.

EasySubli

A Siser HTV product that allows you to sublimate on non-poly or dark blanks.

Gassing Out

A defect during pressing where the ink "bursts out" beyond where it should be, usually caused by the transfer not being taped tightly to the substrate or too much ink on the page.

Ghosting

When a shadow, blur, or "ghost" of your image appears on your substrate. This is often caused by a shift in the design during the heat process.

Glitter HTV

Glitter HTV is a polyester material that can be sublimated. This is a hack for using sublimation on dark or non-polyester fabric blanks.

Heat-Conductive Green Pad

A heat-conductive, metal-infused rubber pad used for pressing projects with beveled edges or slightly irregular surfaces.

Heat Press

A heat press is a piece of equipment needed for transferring a printed image to the blank.

Heat-Resistant Adhesive Spray

A light adhesive that is used in place of heat-resistant tape to keep the sublimation transfer in place while pressing a blank.

Heat-Resistant Gloves

Heat gloves are specialized gloves that protect your hands from hot heat press temperatures.

Heat-Resistant Tape

Heat-resistant tape is used to keep the sublimation transfer in place while pressing a blank.

Heat-Transfer Vinyl (HTV)

Heat-transfer vinyl (HTV or iron-on vinyl) is a material that has a heat-activated adhesive.

High-Heat Foam

Foam used underneath items to flatten out any seams or awkward edges and transfer a design evenly, similar to a pressing pillow.

ICC Profile

A bit of computer code that is specific to a printer, ink, and paper combination. This profile should help with color correction.

Infusible Ink

Infusible Ink is a sublimation product from Cricut. Infusible Ink transfer sheets and pens are made of dry ink, and when high heat is applied, the ink is transferred to the substrate.

Iron-On Vinyl

Iron-on vinyl (also known as heat-transfer vinyl or HTV) is a material that has a heat-activated adhesive.

JPG File

A JPG (or JPEG) is an image file created with pixels. This type of file is typically used for saving photographs.

Mirror

Reversing an image before printing so it sublimates correctly on a blank.

Mug Press

A specialized press designed for making mugs.

Nomex Pad

A thick felt pad used for pressing more-delicate substrates or substrates with beveled edges. Can also protect substrates from "rack lines" in a convection oven.

Nozzle

The part of a printer that disperses the ink onto the paper. See also: Print Heads

Overcooked

When a substrate and transfer are left in a heat press for too long.

Platen

The hot metal plate of a heat press.

PNG File

A PNG is an image file created with pixels. PNGs usually have transparent backgrounds, making them suitable for sublimation printing.

Poly Coating

A special coating applied to substrates to make them suitable for sublimation.

Polyester

An artificial fiber suitable for sublimation.

PolySpray

A spray used to coat a non-polyester blank such as cotton. It coats the fibers in a polyester chemical. Once it dries, you can sublimate on it, but results can vary.

Pre-press

Pressing your blank before you add your transfer sheet to remove wrinkles and moisture.

Pressing Pillow

A covered, heat-resistant piece of foam used underneath items to flatten out any seams or awkward edges and transfer a design evenly.

Press Lines

These lines occur around your image on thin fabrics or with too much pressure. A pressing pillow can be used to minimize press lines.

Press Time

The amount of time your blank is touching the heat press platen. Also called the dwell time.

Pressure

The amount of force/pressure you need to apply to your substrate using your heat source.

Print Heads

The part of a printer that disperses the ink onto the paper. See also: Nozzle

Protective Paper

Paper to protect your heat press and sublimation blanks during heat press process. Most crafters use butcher paper or parchment paper. May also be called blowout paper.

Sandwich

The stacking order for a heat press, which may include the heat press, protective paper, the substrate, the transfer, a rubber pad, and more.

Shrink Wrap

Shrink-wraps are used for items that are hard to press in a regular heat press. The wrap goes around the blank and the item is heated inside a convection oven to create the process of sublimation.

Silicone Wrap

A silicone wrap is used for cylindrical items like water bottles that are hard to press in a regular heat press. The wrap goes around the blank

and the item is heated inside a convection oven to create the process of sublimation.

Speckles

Also called specks, these are little dots that can appear blue or black after pressing your substrate. This is typically caused by lint present on your material before pressing. To avoid specks, use a lint roller before applying your transfer image.

SubliLinen

A specific brand name of a linen-look polyester fabric.

Sublimation

Sublimation is a chemical process where solid ink turns into a gas without going through a liquid stage. When heated, this solid ink turns into a gas, permeates the base material, and then instantly "dries" back into a solid, becoming one with the material.

Sublimation Ink

This is the ink used to print sublimation transfers. When heat and pressure are added, the ink infuses into the blank, creating a permanent, vibrant image.

Sublimation Paper

Specialized paper required for sublimation.

Sublimation Printer

The printer you use to print sublimation transfers. There are sublimation-specific printers, as well as regular printers that

are converted to sublimation printing.

Sublimation Transfer

The printed page out of a sublimation printer. The transfer is used to apply the design to the substrate.

SubliShrink

A specific brand of shrink-wrap used for sublimating unusually shaped items.

Substrate

A substrate is anything you can put a sublimation design on. A few popular substrates include T-shirts, baby bodysuits, tumblers, mugs, and pillows. See also: Blank.

SVG File

An SVG is an image file type popular with crafters who use cutting machines. You can sublimate SVG images.

Templates

Templates are used to size your images properly. You will need a design software to use templates.

Undercooked

When a substrate and transfer are not left long enough to press in the heat press.

Vapor Apparel

100% polyester shirts used for sublimation printing.

Acknowledgments

Another book is, well, in the books! I couldn't have done this without the incredible support of the following folks:

First, I'd like to thank Better Day Books for their guidance and support in bringing my vision to life, and to the generous manufacturers who provided supplies and materials for the projects in this book, including Sawgrass, Heat Transfer Warehouse, Cricut, and PYD Life.

I'd also like to thank my wonderful community of friends for their endless support and troubleshooting when I ran into issues. A special thanks to Angie Holden, Crystal Summers, Amy Motroni, Heidi Kundin, Charynn Olsheski, Cheryl Spangenberg, and Nicole Baker for making me laugh, offering your encouragement, and keeping me focused.

A big thank-you to my parents for helping me with photography and for inviting our boys over to play more times than I can count while I was working hard on finishing up this book.

And to Ryan, Callum, and Sebastian, who are forever supportive of my crafty dreams and who made the space and time in their lives so I could work on bringing this vision to life. You are my world and I love you so much.

Finally, thank you to my amazing community of Hey, Let's Make Stuff readers who have shown me just how popular sublimation crafting can be—you've encouraged me on this sublimation journey more than you'll ever know. It's because of you that I get to live this crafty life, and I am so grateful to each and every one of you.

Happy crafting!